Voices of Michigan...

an Anthology of Michigan's Finest New Authors

First edition
1999

~~~

Foreword by Sue Harrison,
a Michigan author.

Voices of Michigan
MackinacJane's Publishing Company
Box 475
Mackinac Island, Michigan 49757

D0927090

Voices of Michigan...
an Anthology of Michigan's finest new authors

First edition, 1999
First printing, March 1999
Copyright © 1999

Published in the United States of America by
MackinacJane's Publishing Company

Printed in the United States of America by:
Thomson-Shore, Inc.
7300 West Joy Road
Dexter, Michigan 48130-9701

Library of Congress Catalog Number: 98-067911
ISBN: 0-9667363-0-3

Cover ~ Marlee Musser
Cover Design ~ Ceci Floren-Winston
Interior Art ~ Rob Harrell
Title ~ Melinda Hare
Typesetting ~ Juanita Smith
Editing ~ Jane H. Winston
Additional editing by Margaret Howard and Janice Trollinger.

Voices of Michigan
MackinacJane's Publishing Company
Box 475
Mackinac Island, Michigan 49757

This first edition of *Voices of Michigan*

is dedicated to

Irene Y. Walsh
and
Gretchen M. Winston

Both of whom loved Michigan and most especially
Mackinac Island.

Foreword

by
Sue Harrison, a Michigan author

There's an old joke about Michigan that describes our seasons as "nine months of winter and three months of poor sledding." Though we complain, I believe our long winters have given us one of the great treasures of our Michigan heritage -- storytellers and their tales. Who can deny that there is magic inherent in hearth fires and winter winds, in the quietness of snow-laden trees and winter-locked roads, magic that emerges in stories and poems and songs spun fine as frost pasterns?

I grew up in the flat clay plains of the Eastern Upper peninsula, my childhood spanning the fifties and sixties, and overlapping the lives of people who remembered homesteading that land, wresting a living from the fields they claimed from swamps and forest. The land demanded tribute -- paid out in youth and strength and sometimes even life itself -- but in recompense repaid in stories. And so, I heard the histories of those families who came from Canada and England and Scotland and Poland, their toughness, their tenacity. The wells dug by hand, the fields cleared with horse in harness, the crops raised, the children who lived -- and died. Native legends, the first great stories of Michigan, also became a part of my life -- Shinglebiss, Manabozho, the Windigoes.

Later, I would feast on the strident, earthy voices of Ernest Hemingway and Jim Harrison; the rich, honed prose of Stuart Dybeck and Charles Baxter; the wry wisdom of Kathleen Stocking, the fast-paced, intriguing novels of S. K. Wolf; the joyous stories of Priscilla Cogan and Gloria Whelan; the tough, honest novels of Loren Estleman; the soul-touching biographies of Eugene Kennedy; and the stories, poems and histories from other gifted Michigan authors too numerous to mention.

Their diversity is the hallmark of Michigan itself. A diversity of voices, histories and geographies. Their stories bind us to our land and lakes, and make up the whole cloth of life, a fabric defined and delineated by difference and the celebration of that difference

In that same tradition of excellence and diversity, **Voices of Michigan** introduces readers to new writers whose visions incorporated the beauty, honesty and uniqueness of fine literature. Each story and poem contained in these pages speaks to the heart, by transcending place, time and vision to enlarge the past, enrich the present and open a reader's mind to the possibilities of the future.

Join me on this journey into a world revealed by new voices well worth hearing, visions that lead us out of ourselves and into the unity and diversity that is Michigan.

~Sue Harrison's novels include *The Ivory Carver Trilogy: Mother Earth Father Sky, My Sister the Moon* and *Brother Wind*; a young adult novel *Sisu; The Storyteller Trilogy: Song of the River, Cry of the Wind,* and to be released in the year 2000: *Call Down The Stars.*

Acknowledgment

This project, a latent dream of mine for years, could never have reached fruition without the help of "bizzilions" of friends and colleagues, and I applaud them all:

Without **Paul Cossman of Humpus Bumpus Books** in Cumming, Georgia there would be no *Voices of Michigan*. Paul and his book contest, *O, Georgia,* were the inspiration and model for our Michigan contest. Thanks, Paul, for being there for us when we needed you. Thanks, also, to my husband, **John T. Winston,** my business partner, **Mary Jane Barnwell,** and her husband **Roman.** What a feeling of satisfaction as we hold in our hands the fruits of our labor!

Additional thanks to **Juanita Smith,** the typist and typesetter as well as friend and colleague from Fort Valley State University where we are both employed;**Ceci Floren-Winston,** a first cousin and the cover designer;**Marlee Musser,** the creator of the oil painting, *Mackinac Dream,* used for the cover; to the **McIntire family,** owners of the **Iroquois Hotel** on Mackinac Island, for granting us permission to use the Musser painting which hangs in the dining room of their hotel; **Rob Harrell** the interior artist; and **Melinda Hare,** the inspiration for the book title.

And thank-yous are also extended to**Margaret Howard, Sue Harrison, Harold Harrell, Fran Barnwell, Diane** and **Joe Brandonisio, Tamara Tomac, Elizabeth Bradley,** all employees of the Island Bookstore in Mackinaw City and on Mackinac Island and to the staff of the Mackinac Island post office.

Thanks to those who served as readers/judges:**Dr. Chris Hauge, Bonnie Sperry, Don McGraw III, Dr. Francis Strauss II, Barbara Schroeder, Kay Beth Harrell, Diane Orth, Glen Young, Lorabeth Fitzgerald, Jean Beardsley Allen, Virginia Garland, Janet Rathke, Doyle Spence** and **Janice Trollinger.**

And finally, thanks to all of you who love writing as much as I do and entered our contest. Congratulations to those who were selected. Never give up writing. Send us your manuscript for next year's contest today!!

~Jane H. Winston, editor

Contents

Poetry:

Appendices:

Fiction

West Main Street

Voices of Michigan

Antlers in the Treetops

Maurice C. McGleish

I knew this winter was going to be different. There were subtle clues such as an early frost followed by light snow showers in early October. Animals were busy stockpiling huge amounts of food which we supplied for them. And of course, the ever-knowing weather forecasters were predicting a mild winter, a sure guarantee of anything but a mild winter.

But we were ready. We had already built a large pen which now housed our first pair of Siberian Huskies. They had an uncanny resemblance to wolves but would be raised to be used as sled dogs. These dogs were intelligent and extremely alert. They were quick to let us know when anyone or anything came on our property.

Maurice C. McGleish was born in Detroit. He is retired from the U.S. Air Force. He and his wife, Shirley, raise Siberian Huskies and enjoy dog sledding.

The first snowstorm started in October, continuing on a daily basis, and by Christmas Eve we had exceeded the total snowfall of the previous year. There was almost three feet of snow on the roof of the house, and some of it had melted and turned into ice.

But this evening, no one seemed to care. After all, it was Christmas time. We celebrated by having our usual Christmas Eve dinner followed by the passing of gifts. And

3

there was so many of them that they wouldn't all fit under the tree.

After all, wasn't that what Christmas was about? Go out and spend your money on all kinds of gifts - the more expensive the better. Then Christmas is forgotten until the following year.

The past several years I had wished that Christmas had some real meaning like it did when I was a kid. It wasn't enjoyable like I remembered. But more than that, something was missing and I couldn't put my finger on it. Of course, everyone knew there was no such thing as Santa Claus. Even our youngest son knew that I was the family Santa because I provided the money for all the gifts.

Why did it have to become commercialized like everything else, I thought as I climbed into bed and fell into an immediate deep sleep. I awoke to a muffled thud on our roof. As I lay there trying to figure out what the noise was, I heard the jingling of bells accompanied by a voice whispering, "Quiet. You don't want to wake these folks up."

Almost immediately, as if on cue, our pair of huskies began barking loudly.

Now wide awake, I sat up in bed, "What's going on out there?" *I'd better check this out.*

Before my feet could touch the floor, there was a swishing sound on the roof, followed by a loud crashing noise and the jingling of bells in the trees near the end of the house.

I dressed hurriedly, donned my boots and coat, and proceeded out the front door.

As I looked toward the end of the house, I saw our two dogs standing at one corner of the pen looking up into the trees. Not that this was unusual; they were always staring at

4

the birds and squirrels high up in the branches. However, their deep growls told me that all was not right out there.

Walking around the corner of the house, I looked up and stopped in my tracks. I could not believe what I was seeing. Hanging in the branches of one of our large maple trees was a big sleigh with eight deer in harnesses suspended in midair.

As I stood there dumbfounded by this sight, I was startled by a voice coming from underneath the tree. "What a fine kettle of fish."

There sitting in the snow was a short robust figure of a man. He was covered with snow and broken pieces of branches. As he stood up and began to brush himself off, I could see part of a red suit trimmed with white protruding from the top of the flight suit he was wearing.

"Any chance I can get some help with my reindeer?" asked the little man.

"Pardon," I said.

"I need to unhook my reindeer before they hurt themselves."

"How," I asked, as I watched the deer struggling to remain airborne.

"Well, if you've got a ladder, I can climb up and unhook the reins and harness from the sleigh."

"I've got one in the barn. Just a moment," I said as I took off around the house.

I returned with my extension ladder which we propped up against the tree, and the little man gingerly scampered up to the top rung and reached out toward the sleigh.

"I can't quite reach them. How about a hand."

I climbed the ladder to the rung just below the man.

At slightly over six feet, I was able to reach my arm around him and unloosen the reins and harness from the sleigh.

"Okay. Walk down the ladder and hang onto the reins until I get down," he said. I climbed down the ladder followed by my visitor. When he reached the ground, he took the reins from me and walking toward an open area behind the house, he said, "Now Dasher, now Prancer...." All of a sudden the reindeer lunged forward and up into the sky, pulling the little man off his feet and dropping him in a snow bank. "Oh no! Get back here you guys," he yelled disgustingly as he crawled out of the snow bank.

"What's the matter with them," I asked.

"Don't worry, they'll be back. How about giving me a hand with the sleigh."

"I don't know. That thing looks pretty heavy to me."

"It is. Especially when it's loaded. Thank goodness none of the cargo fell out."

"Cargo?"

"Of course. I make this run every year about this time. This is one of my first stops. Well, it has been a number of years since I've been here. Thought I would give it a try this year. Never mind, you'll understand. Right now, we need to get that sleigh down."

"We could try calling the auto club, they might be able to help."

"Do they know anything about handling sleighs?"

"Not sure. We can call and find out. Come on inside."

"Think I'll stay here in case those confounded deer come back."

"Okay," I said as I headed toward the front door.

6

"They spook every time they get around wolves. Didn't realize there were any in this area."

"They're not wolves, they're Huskies. We just got them this summer. Sorry if they caused any problems."

"First time this has happened in several hundred years."

*Several hundred....*naw, I don't want to ask.

I went into the house, fumbled to get my membership card out of my wallet, and dialed the auto club number.

What am I doing, I thought while I waited for a representative to answer. *Come on Herb, wake up before you begin to believe this is really happening to....*

"Auto club. How can I help you?"

"Uh, I'd like to request assistance for a disabled vehicle."

"May I have your membership number please?"

"3759900299100."

"And your name, sir?"

"Herb Swanson."

"Where is the vehicle located, Mr. Swanson?"

"Beside my house."

"What seems to be the problem, sir?"

"Well, it's kinda' stuck."

"In the snow?"

"Not so much in the snow, but rather over it."

"Can't you dig it out of the snow?"

"No. It's caught in a big branch."

"I beg your pardon?"

"It's stuck in a branch."

"Can't you cut the branch loose?"

"Not really."

"Why not?"

"It's too high off the ground."

"Off the ground?"

"Yes ma'am."

"The branch or the vehicle is off the ground?"

"Both."

"The vehicle is off the ground?"

"It fell off my roof."

"Your roof? I'm almost scared to ask this. How did it get on your roof?"

"It landed there."

"Oh, I see. It's a plane then?"

"Not quite."

"A helicopter?"

"Not really."

"Mr. Swanson, what kind of vehicle landed on your roof?"

"A sleigh."

"What? Sir, is this some sort of crank call?"

"No ma'am. There's a sleigh stuck in the tree beside my house and I need help getting it down."

"Sir, I don't think your membership covers sleighs."

"Why not? It's a vehicle, isn't it?"

"Just a moment sir, let me talk to my supervisor."

The phone clicked as I was put on hold. *They'll think I'm crazy and cancel my insurance.*

Just then a different voice came on the line. "Mr. Swanson, my name is Mr. Frost and...."

Not Jack Frost, I hope.

". . . I understand a sleigh landed on your roof, fell off and got caught in a tree beside your house, is that correct?"

"Yes. And I'm not crazy, and this isn't a crank call. I really need some help moving this thing."

"Okay. Quite honestly, we've never run into this kind of situation before. I'm going to put you on hold a moment while we research this matter."

Click. *They think I'm nuts.*

After several minutes the phone clicked again. "Mr. Swanson, your situation is extremely unusual to say the least. I'm not sure how we could categorize this. How far from your house is the sleigh?"

"About ten feet."

"Do you feel it would present a danger to your home and family if it were to fall right now?"

"You bet it would."

"Okay. We're going to cover this under your homeowner's policy and call it a safety hazard. I'll have our dispatcher contact a road crew in your area and have them dispatch a vehicle to your home."

Yeah, a wagon with men in white coats, I'll bet.

"But sir, if this turns out to be a false alarm, you will be responsible for all costs incurred by this situation, not to mention having your policy reviewed."

"That's great. You really won't be sorry, I'll guarantee you that much."

"I hope not."

"The whole world's depending on your help." *What made me say that?*

"Sure Mr. Swanson. You have a good night. Oh, and Merry Christmas."

Have a good night? It's two-thirty in the morning.

About an hour later a truck with a large crane pulled

into the driveway. The window on the driver's side of the truck rolled down and a tired unshaven face looked down at me. "You the guy with something in a tree?"

"That's me, and I'm sure glad you're here."

The driver got out of the vehicle and followed me around the end of the house.

I pointed up. "There she is."

The man gawked and his eyes opened wide in disbelief. "How did this happen?"

"I don't think you want to know."

"You're probably right."

This new arrival stood there viewing the situation for a moment, then he walked around the tree. "I think we might be able to handle this," he said.

After about two hours of maneuvering the truck, crane and cables, the driver was able to get the sleigh free and lowered to the ground.

The little man in the flight suit who had been watching discreetly from the corner of the house walked up to the driver. "Any chance you can put the sleigh back up on the house?"

"Don't push it," I cautioned.

He quietly nodded his head in agreement.

I signed the emergency assistance slip, thanked the man for coming out and watched as he drove out of the drive, his face still bearing a puzzled look.

I turned to the little man. "What next?"

"My reindeer came back. I've got them behind the house. It's going to be difficult hooking them back up."

"Why's that?"

"If I bring them back here to the sleigh, your wolves

are going to spook them again. My deer just don't take kindly to those critters."

"I told you, they're not wolves."

"Tell that to my reindeer. They think they are."

"I've got an idea. Let's see if we can pull the sleigh out to the driveway with my truck. After that, you can bring the deer around the far side of the house, and then we can hook them back up to the sleigh."

Half an hour later the deer were once again connected to the sleigh which was now parked in the driveway. The little man thanked me for my help. "Have a Merry Christmas and a Happy New Year."

I was suddenly overcome by a strange feeling. I remembered what Christmas was about when I was a child, and that it really didn't have to change when we became adults.

He then climbed in his sleigh, to his team gave a whistle. They ran down the drive like wind-borne thistle. And I heard him exclaim as he flew out of sight, "I'm going home, what a harrowing night."

Voices of Michigan

King of the Forest

Tom Hoover

The thing that makes me happy started with the very first boat ride I ever took. Daddy told me all about what was gonna happen. About how we'd drive for a long, long time and finally we'd drive right on up to a boat and the boat'd take us over the water to the place where the deer waited for us to shoot them. I got scared about the boat but Daddy said it was okay 'cause it was a big, safe boat and I told him I wasn't scared. But I was.

> **Tom Hoover** has lived in Michigan for 20 years having come from Kokomo, Indiana. He lives with his wife, Eileen, and daughter, Zoe. This is his first writing contest, but *not* his last story.

My big brother Will was all mad for weeks and weeks 'cause Daddy said I was to come on the trip, and Will said the best thing could happen was if I got shot 'cause I'm slow and ain't much use. I don't think I'll get shot 'cause Daddy showed me how to work my gun and never to point it at anybody even Will 'cause he hates me. Daddy sometimes looks like he wants to shoot Will but he never does because you're only supposed to shoot deer. But sometimes he hits Will and then Will hits me late at night with a rag stuffed in my mouth so I don't make noise. Then Will says he's gonna shoot us all some day and when I tell him *Daddy says you only shoot deer* Will hits me some more.

We waited and waited and finally Daddy said we were going the next day. Mommy cried and said *please be careful*

13

Frank, you know he forgets all the time . . . . I just don't know.
Daddy looked like something was hurting him and said,
*Christ, Martha, we can't shelter the boy all his life. He's sixteen
now - gotta' start gettin' him ready for the real world.* Then
Mommy cried some more. I told her it was gonna be okay.
That I wouldn't shoot myself. Will said, *Fat chance.* Mommy
started screaming really loud at Will and I went to bed so I
could get under the covers and go to sleep. Mommy and
Daddy and Will all yelled for a long time and I didn't sleep
until everything was quiet. Then Dad was waking me up and
he smelled like beer and it was the start of when I was happy
'cause the beer smell made me happy 'cause I knew we were
going to shoot deer.

    We drove and drove. Will got to drive the car for a
while and he was real nice. Daddy slept in the back of the car
and Will let me play the radio. He wouldn't let me use
Daddy's special phone to call Mommy 'cause he said, *You'll
just get her cryin' an' it'll ruin the whole weekend so don't ask me
anymore an' don't ask Pop.* I pretended to talk to Mommy on
the phone, and Will got mad and made me turn off the radio.
I went to sleep and when I woke up Daddy was driving. He
said we were almost there and for me to start looking for deer.
I looked and looked but didn't see any and the looking made
me a little sick so I stopped.

    Soon we came to the place where the boat was, and I
got real scared 'cause Dad drove the car right up on the boat.
I guess I was yelling a lot 'cause Will kept yelling at me to shut
up, and then Daddy got real mad and started yelling at me,
but he stopped when a guy came up to the car and asked us to
get out. Daddy and Will got out real fast, but I had some
trouble 'cause my door got locked, and I couldn't work it right

14

until Daddy came over and told me to *do it easy, just pull up on the button and push.* I got out and walked with Dad and Will to a little room where Will said we had to wait until the boat got moving. I really liked sitting there 'cause outside there were lots of scary dogs that Daddy said guys used to look for deer and Will said isn't that illegal and Daddy said it was okay 'cause the law don't count on the island. They talked and talked while we sat in the little room waiting to go.

A man sat across from me and he had a little brown dog inside his coat that looked at me like he wanted to play, but I knew I better not 'cause the man didn't tell me it was okay. The man asked me some things about deer and if I hunted and other stuff. When I told him about my gun and about Daddy telling me to not shoot anybody but deer, the man laughed and let me pet his dog. The dog licked my fingers and it felt tickly and his tongue was real fast and pink. The dog was real shaky and his tail moved his whole butt back and forth and it made me laugh. I was real happy.

Daddy and Will stopped talking and Will decided to go look at the dogs, but I stayed inside with Daddy 'cause I was holding the man's dog, and he was licking my hand and pushing it like he was looking for something. The man was asleep. Daddy told me about the deer again and where to shoot it and what to do when it was dead and how happy Mommy would be when we all got back. He got out his face paint, and I got excited 'cause I forgot all about the face paint 'cause Daddy got mad last week when I painted up my face and scared Mommy, and he told me not to touch it again until it was time. Daddy put the paint on his face and it made him look really scary and his eyes bugged out and his teeth looked really big. Then he gave the paint to me and let me

15

paint my face. When I got done Daddy got out a little mirror and let me look at my face. I wasn't scary at all. It was just me with paint on.

The man woke up and the little dog started shaking and making noises like he was glad the man was awake. He jumped out of my coat and went to the man who scratched his ears and the man talked to him about going out to see the big dogs. Daddy said the man better not 'cause the big dogs would eat the little dog with just one bite. The man laughed and went outside. I saw the little dog later, so he must not have got ate.

Will came back and he smelled like beer and Daddy let him paint his face just like us. Daddy laughed a lot and put his arm around Will saying *this is how it should be, son! This is going to be great! You'll see!* Will smiled a lot and gave me the paints to hold.

Then Daddy got up and told me to come along. We went out to see the big dogs and the other people's cars. The boat was very dark and it was cold. Daddy took me to the side and showed me the water and showed me where we were going, but I didn't see nothing because it was a black night. Daddy told me to try not to say much to Will 'cause he was mad 'cause you come, but that's okay cause you're gonna' be our good luck. I told Daddy I didn't know what luck was, and he said don't worry it's just something good that I got. So I watched the men with the big dogs smoking and being loud and drinking beer. Daddy didn't say much. It was getting cold, so I asked if we could go back inside and Daddy said sure.

Will was there and he was talking to the man with the little dog. The boat started to make some noises and I got

16

scared. Will laughed and said maybe we were sinking. I asked Daddy what sinking was and he said, *Never mind, and you shut up Will.* Then a big man with a beard came in the little room and said we were gonna' land soon and to get to our cars. We went out and all the dogs were barking and the other men were laughing and yelling at their dogs. I got in the car but Will and Daddy stood outside. I could see them yelling at each other until Will got in and slammed the door real hard and yelled at me. He said a bunch of bad words especially the "F" one. Then he got quiet. The boat bumped against something really hard and Will said, *Shit!* Daddy got in and started the car. I looked but I didn't see no road. I asked Daddy where the road was, but he didn't say. He held on the steering wheel like he was driving, but I could tell the car wasn't moving. I looked and we were still on the boat. I started to get scared, but I wasn't that scared so I had fun.

The big man with the beard came and told Daddy to *get ready after the pickup.* Daddy waited a little while and then he drove right off the boat!

We drove and drove. Daddy kept telling me to look out for deer. It was very dark so I didn't see none. Will fell asleep and was squishing me against the door. I wasn't sleepy at all. Daddy talked to himself a lot. *Is this it? Yeah. Yeah. Right here . . . then left. Here we go!* We finally stopped and Daddy turned the car off. It was real dark. Like when I hide in the laundry closet in the basement when Will chases me. And real quiet. Daddy sat still for a while and I thought we were all going to sleep right in the car. Will was snoring and Daddy hit him on the shoulder to wake him up.

"Get up Will! We gotta' make camp!"

Will grumbled and moaned. Then he pushed me out

the door.

Daddy gave me and Will flashlights and I could see trees all around us. There was a big field where the car was, and I didn't see no road. The light made neat colors on the trees and I shook my light to make them change. I stopped when Daddy told me to *stop screwing around and start getting the sleeping bags out.*

I got all the bags out. I had trouble with Will's because he ties knots real hard. Daddy and Will got the big tent up and I was glad because I was tired and a little scared because it was real quiet and my flashlight was making things look weird. I had to go potty, but I tried to hold it. I got in my sleeping bag and tried not to think about how I had to go. I sure didn't want to go in the dark. Daddy told me goodnight and for me to dream about deer, but I hoped I would dream about candy.

I fell asleep but I woke up later. My tummy hurt because it was full of pee and I couldn't hold it no more so I went right outside the tent with my flashlight. I went fast and I got some on my jammies, but it was okay. It wasn't much. I got done and I went back to the tent. Daddy and Will were outside sitting by a little fire. They were talking and drinking beer. Will was being real loud like when he'd get mad and start hitting me. I went to sleep so I wouldn't hear him no more. Right before I fell asleep, I could hear Will sayin' I was gonna ruin his hunting. I knew I liked to hunt, but I didn't know what ruin was. I knew I'd better not do it because Will wouldn't like it.

I didn't dream about nothing and when I woke up I knew it was morning time even though I couldn't see any light. The paint on my face itched real bad but I didn't scratch 'cause Daddy said I had to hide real good all the time to shoot a deer. And paint kept you hid real good.

I got up real quiet. Daddy was snoring but I didn't see Will. I had to pee again and I couldn't wait so I went right outside in just my jammies. It was real cold and the pee wouldn't come and then it did. While I was going a big deer with lots of horns come out around our car. He had big horns like the kind Daddy said were good for shooting. The deer looked at me and snorted like he had a cold or something. I got quiet and got on tippy-toes. I snuck back to the tent. The big deer watched me. He looked like he wanted to play.

Daddy was still asleep so I had to be extra quiet and that was hard 'cause I wanted to wake Daddy up and ask him what I should do. But I didn't. Daddy would shoot the deer so that's what I was gonna do. I got my gun out from Daddy's big case and loaded it with the special bullets that Daddy said were "deer dum-dums." I didn't see how bullets could be dumb, but that's just what Daddy called them. I didn't push the little button called the safety button. Daddy said I should never push this button when the gun had bullets in it except if I was with him or I was gonna shoot a deer. I peeked out of the tent and the big deer was still there. Right by the car. Then I heard Daddy rustle around behind me. He said, *What the hell are you doing?* and I told him, real quiet like, *There's a deer right outside, Dad.* And Daddy said, *Go get'em son, I'll be with you. Be real quiet and slow now!* I pushed the button in on the gun and tippy-toed outside.

The deer was far away now, but he was still looking at me. I went real slow. It was hard 'cause the gun got real heavy and I was shaking 'cause of the cold. I looked at the deer down the rifle like Daddy showed me, and I saw the spot

19

on the deer where the rifle would make him dead and I looked real, real hard. The I closed my finger on the trigger and pushed and pushed and the gun went off. It hit me hard in the shoulder and hurt bad so I dropped it right away. The deer jumped up funny off the ground. Straight up and then it fell and didn't move.

Daddy yelled and grabbed me and hugged me hard. I couldn't breathe good 'cause Daddy was squeezing me and I wanted him to let go so I could go look at the deer. Then Daddy let go of me and I saw he was crying, and I asked him what was wrong. He shook his head and said, *Let's go look at your deer.* He didn't yell at me for dropping the gun or being outside in my jammies. He was happy and I was happy.

We were almost to the deer when Will popped up out of the woods. He was far away, and yelling something. Daddy yelled back, *Get on over here and see the deer Junior just shot!* Will yelled the *F* word real loud, and he pointed his rifle at where the deer was. He shot his gun and I heard Daddy make a funny sound and he fell to the ground just like the deer.

After that I got real, real scared and I guess I was so scared I didn't notice Will come up and start hollering at me to go get Daddy's phone. Will hit me a few times and I went and got the phone. When I got back Daddy was sitting up and holding a big wad of something on his shoulder. There was a lot of blood, and I started crying and saying that Will tried to shoot Daddy. Will tried to hit me again and Daddy told him to *cut it out goddammit! Gimme that phone!*

Daddy tried and tried to use his phone but it wouldn't work so he told Will to go get the car and drive it over. While we waited Daddy made me cut the insides out of the deer and it was real bad. I cried and my tummy threw up a lot, but after I got done Daddy said he was real proud of me and that Will did try to shoot him. I asked if Will was going to jail, but Daddy was moaning a lot and Will finally came with the car.

Daddy yelled at Will and told him to help me get the deer in the trunk. Will was crying and saying *I'm sorry* all the time. The deer was too big and we had to leave the trunk open. Daddy got in the front and he was acting like he was real tired like when he drinks a lot of beer. Will drove real fast. I wasn't crying no more but Will was crying a lot. He drove real bad and I got scared 'cause we went off the road a few times and Daddy would yell, *Jesus Christ!* Then Will would say he was sorry again and then he'd drive better.

We finally got to the place where the big boat was and Daddy wasn't awake any more. Will told me to *sit right where I was and don't you dare move.* He got out and ran to the boat and he came right back with the big man with the beard and some other men. They woke up my Daddy, but he wasn't talking right. The big man said he'd get Charlie and they'd fly out to the hospital. I couldn't say anything I was so scared and when they helped my Daddy into another car they wouldn't let me come and I cried and cried.

Then the man with the little dog came and we went to a place where he gave me hot chocolate. It was really hot with lots of marshmallows like I like it. His little dog sat in my lap and ate marshmallows off my fingers. He was real careful and didn't bite me. The man told me that Will and my Daddy had to go right to the doctors and that my Mommy would be here in a few hours to look after me. He asked me about the deer and I told him how I shot it and the man laughed and laughed. The deer was up on a big pole by the big boat and I could see it right outside. A lot of people were looking at it. I asked Mike (that's his name) what I should do with the deer. Daddy never said how to eat it or nothing. It looked too big for me to eat all by myself. Mike laughed some more and said not to worry about it. He said the deer was the biggest one he'd ever seen and that the DNR was going to come measure it and give me a prize. I didn't know what the DNR was, but I really like surprises and felt better and didn't miss my Daddy so much. Mike said the deer was the king of the forest. He said now I was the king. I said I couldn't be 'cause I wasn't a deer and I didn't want to live outside all the time. Mike laughed again and I got tired and he let me lay down right there. His little dog sat right by my head and his fur tickled my nose a little before I fell asleep.

I dreamed about the little dog and he could talk. He said I was king of the forest and I shouldn't be afraid. He said it was okay because I was retarded and that was good. Then he told me I should wake up and I did. My Mommy was there, and she cried a little and hugged me real tight. I took her to see my deer and then she cried some more when she saw it and said, *So now the bastard's got you doing it too.* She grabbed my hand and took me to the dock. We got on a small boat and went over the water for a long time. My Mommy didn't say anything to me. She held my hand real tight even when we sat in the room where the driver was.

They wouldn't let me see my Daddy at the doctors but Mommy let me have some money and told me how to get candy out of the machines. I waited by myself in a big room with lots of other people. They all looked sad or mad or scared. I ate four Butterfingers.

Then we went home but Daddy didn't come for a long

time. We went to the hospital where he stayed because he was sick and couldn't move. I talked to him a lot and he talked to me, but he talked funny like when he watches football too long and falls asleep in his chair. Mommy said he'll talk like that all the time and to be patient. Will was gone for a while to jail, but he came back and he's all different with new hair and he doesn't hit me. He helps Daddy get round the house, but Daddy gets mad and starts yelling stuff we can't understand and Will gets real quiet. But he doesn't hit me any more. And that makes me happy.

One day a man in a green uniform came with a big box for me and it was the deer I shot. Well, not the whole deer. Just the head. And there was a letter from the DNR that my Mommy read and she said she was proud of me and, she tried to show the letter to Will but he said he had to go do the laundry. The letter said *the deer was the biggest documented buck ever shot in the state* and asked me to be on TV. I asked Mommy if I could and she said of course, and she cried and said she had to go read the letter to Daddy. I went and told Will I was going to be on TV, and he said, *Good for you, and I'm sorry,* again.

And I said, *You sure say that a lot.* And he wouldn't say anything. He acted like he wanted to cry, but I wasn't sure.

I went upstairs to watch football with Daddy and to look at my deer. It's right up on the wall by the TV. I pretend sometimes at night that I'm riding him like a horse and all the animals come out to see me like in the *Lion King* only I'm the one who's the king. And I have adventures with Will and Daddy and Mommy and I'm real, real happy.

Voices of Michigan

The Virgin in the Volkswagen Bus

John H. Kenyon III

The VW bus seemed to slow, ever so slightly, as it rumbled by. Then I saw the brake lights go on, heard a crunching down-shift and watched as she pulled off onto the shoulder of the road.

John Kenyon is a physician's assistant who works exclusively in the open-heart surgery program in Petoskey. He was born and raised in Detroit and graduated from Eastern Michigan. He has lived in Harbor Springs for 25 years with his wife.

"Finally," I mumbled, rising off my suitcase. "A ride."

Hitchhiking outside Grayling on that fall Friday -- the wind whispering winter, the sun a twilight ember in the cloud-streaked sky -- had made me cold, discouraged and itching with impatience. Like a balm, the bus offered a soothing salvation. I groped for the suitcase handle, all the while willing the tail lights closer as she backed toward me. Her brakes screeched a metal-on-metal song, and the sputtering idle of the bus told me she'd stopped. I was just reaching for the passenger door handle when the side-door snapped and slid open.

"This way," she announced. "Can't open the front doors. Toss the suitcase on the bed in the back."

She lunged back to the driver's seat, gunned the

faltering engine, then looked back over her shoulder at me. I bounced the suitcase onto the bed, slid the side-door home and turned to look at her.

"Up here," she smiled, "and don't mind the dog. He's quite deaf, but harmless." Nodding to the passenger seat, she fairly shouted, "Toker! Toker! Bed!"

A sizeable grey/black dog of indeterminate parentage obediently climbed down off the seat, gave me a perfunctory sniff as he trod by, and resolutely climbed up onto the bed, nuzzling and sniffing at my suitcase.

As I settled into the dog-warmed seat, she revved the engine, released the clutch, and the bus haltingly broke loose of the shoulder gravel and bumped onto the highway. Moments later, whining, jostling, and swaying, the bus snuck up to 65.

"Sign on your suitcase says 'E. Lansing'. Well, I'm headed to Ann Arbor with stops in Mt. Pleasant and East Lansing," she said softly, her voice trailing off. "If you don't mind laying over in Mt. Pleasant for an hour or so, I can take you all the way."

"No problem. Just happy to be on the road again. 'preciate the lift."

"Name's Skilly," she said, glancing at me.

Skilly? I asked myself, wondering if I'd heard it right.

"Mine's Tom, but I go by TC."

"Yeah. Well, my real name's Michele, but my grandfather nicknamed me Skilly.... after Skil-a-galee. It's a lighthouse on a shoal in Lake Michigan." She paused. "My grandad was a lighthouse keeper around the Lakes and his last posting was there...at Skilly..." Again her voice trailed off and her profiled face seemed to soften.

In the dimming light of the October evening sky, I really looked at her for the first time. She was cute but not pretty: clear skin, dark eyes, long sandy-brown hair, her nose in profile a trifle long, her jaw slightly squared. Her body was hidden in a long-sleeve blue flannel shirt, well-worn, bell-bottom jeans and scuffed moccasins. Her hands, firmly gripping the steering wheel, bore no rings and showed short, unpolished nails.

"Tell me, um, TC, you going to MOO-U for the big game?" she asked, turning her face slightly toward me and offering up a smile.

"Yeah."

The annual gridiron battle between Michigan and Michigan State would reconvene tomorrow at Spartan Stadium in East Lansing. Taken by the tradition, I usually listened to the game on radio but never attended one. This year would be different. My friend Hack, in his 2nd year at MSU, had called and said he actually had tickets, saying also that he was throwing a post-game party at his pad that promised "beer, broads and bullshit, TC, whether we win or lose." How could I turn him down?

"So what are you doing thumbin' out of Grayling? That your home? How long were you waiting for a ride? Do you really like football? Say, what's your sign?" The flurry of questions startled me, surprised me, and almost left her breathless.

"Hmmm, let's see: I got a ride from my lab partner. He dropped me off in Grayling and went home to Alpena for the weekend. I sat there on US 27 for an hour-and-a-half 'til you came along. Yeah, I love football, my home's in Empire, and I was born in September. So, that make me a Virgo?"

"Depends. What day of the month?" she asked, interest piquing her voice.

"The 4th."

"Makes you a Virgo, same as me. Mine's the 7th." She paused as she turned on the bus's headlights. "So where do you go to school? Obviously not MSU."

"True. I'm at Northwestern Michigan in Traverse City. A junior college."

"You mean there's a JC in TC, TC?" she laughed. "Never heard of it. I go to Michigan Tech. Geology major."

"Don't have a major," I replied. "Kinda' just shopping around." Then I got this feeling I sometimes get: a little burning twinge at the base of my skull whenever questions outnumber my answers. Here I am with a geology Techie who's driving to Ann Arbor with stops in Mt. Pleasant and Lansing. Why? Rock research? Geological gumshoeing?

"So what's in Ann Arbor?" I asked, hoping for a clue.

"I'm delivering stuff, that's all," she said with a finality that left me clueless.

A Zodiac virgin going from Tech to Central to MSU to U of M. And delivering what? Rocks? Socks? Dope? Hope? The twinge in my skull burned on.

Twilight had given way to darkness and the bus hammered along, tunneling its dim headlights into the black beyond. Like miners in a shaft, we chipped away the miles, one light-length at a time.

Mt. Pleasant. We took the 2nd exit and lurched our way through stop lights, stop signs and yields, the bus fading and faltering when forced to idle. Finally, she found Brocken Street, turned left and stopped near the middle of the block in front of a small brick house.

"This is gonna take about an hour, TC. Um, I'd take you in with me, but, um, Karl is a little paranoid, and, um, he doesn't like strangers, and ..."

"It's OK. Really," I said, hoping to intercept another 'um....' "I'll just catch some zzz's."

"If Toker wakes up, you can let him out to do his business. He'll come right back."

That said, she reached under her seat and pulled out a small package, maybe half the size of a shoe box, wrapped neatly in newspaper. She moved to the side-door, opened it, stepped out and slammed the door shut. From my window, I watched as she walked slowly up the sidewalk and onto the darkened porch. Without knocking, she simply opened the door and walked in.

Bathed in darkness and creeping chill, I turned up my coat collar and hunkered down into the seat. From the back of the bus came the rhythmic, raspy snoring of the dog. Up front, the scent of Skilly, mixed with a growing infusion of burned-leaf air, nudged me into thought. *What the hell, I could be standing out on 27 right now, freezing my ass and only hoping for a ride.* If I can hang here for an hour, it's on to East Lansing and... My reverie was broken by a snort, a grunt and the presence of Toker at my side.

"Hey there, Toker. Bet you want out."

My door wouldn't open, so out the side-door the two of us slipped into the autumn night. The dog, probably with a growing familiarity, padded slowly and softly toward some bushes at the side of the small brick house. I tagged along, suddenly aware of a common goal. The dog perched three-legged and I unzipped. Man and dog unleashed small torrents that crackled and steamed in the crisp air. Tucking, then turning, I zipped as I walked back toward the bus, the dog a few steps behind. A man's laugh, quickly followed by, "Freddie will love it," burst forth from the house and stopped me for a moment. Then the dog brushed past me, thoroughly deaf to events in the house, hinting that I pursue his example.

We waited for almost an hour; the dog on the bed, me in the passenger seat with my eyes fixed on the house. When she emerged, literally bouncing off the porch and almost skipping down the walk, I feigned sleep. Without a word she climbed in, started the bus, and was out of Mt. Pleasant, heading south, before I un-feigned my nap.

"Where are we?" I asked pseudogroggily.

"On 27, maybe an hour from Lansing," she answered, her voice thick but steady. "Say, TC, do you smoke? You know, smoke, uh, pot?"

"Rarely," I lied. Actually, I had been stoned just once, with a certain Jennifer Howard, a lithe and loony one-time date who possessed an explosive glandular passion that detonated only when she and her consort were helplessly high. Ah, sweet Jennifer, she of the comely smile and the bed post notched in tribute to the parade of men she had bedded (I became number 23, literally notched, as were 22 others). Sweet Jennifer, she of the...

"Well, Karl rolled me a couple and I'm having some. Care to join in?"

With that, she lit one, drew deeply once or twice, and

passed it to me. Wary though willing, I took a toke and re-passed it. She drew again, and when I shook my head 'no' as she offered it back, she snubbed it out. That's when I noticed the ring on her right hand.

Doubt, that demon of discord, twinged warmly at the base of my skull. Had I missed it earlier? Did she get it in Mt. Pleasant? Did she take it out of her pocket? Did she...

"Interesting ring," I remarked, though barely able to see it.

"SDS ring," she said flatly.

"What?" I blurted, thinking she said FDS ring and imagining a fruited-fragranced, fine-mist spray jetting into her nether regions from some mechanistic magic on her finger.

"Actually, it's an SDS founder's ring. It's Karl's. He gave it to me for luck." She held up her hand as if to study it. "Know about the SDS?" Her voice was almost a taunt, and it goaded me to dredge the channels of my memory. SDS?

Students for a Democratic Society. A radical cadre of college kids fomenting revolution on campuses all over the country. Anti-war, anti-authority, anti-establishment: the very personification of the 60's.

"Heard about 'em but don't know anyone," I slurred, the single hit of marijuana now ballooning my tongue and parching my throat. "Little too far out for me."

"Figures," I think she said, almost at a whisper.

Suddenly, Skilly stomped on the brakes and swung the steering wheel hard left, pitching me out of my seat. My forehead slapped the unforgiving dash, my head snapped back, and through hazed eyes I caught a glimpse of the unmoving deer as we barely grazed by it.

"Stupid deer.   TC, you OK?" she asked, alarm touching her voice.

"Argh," I managed, clutching my head with both hands. "Holy sh...."

"Want me to pull over? You OK?" she repeated, alarm growing in her voice.

"Wha...." I gurgled, consciousness ebbing and flowing in my addled brain like driftwood in a tidal pool.

"You're hurt!" she shrieked, slowing and jockeying the bus to a stop at the edge of the road.

"Oh, man, I'm sorry. Couldn't hit the deer. Jesus, TC, let me have a look."

She flipped open the glove box, took out a flashlight, clicked it on and fired a bullet of light into my face.

"Oh, shit," she groaned, grabbing a wad of paper napkins from the glove box, then pressing them to my head. "Say something, TC."

Dazed, doped but determined, I gave it my best shot.

"Mist da deer. Close. 'ood job," I garbled.

"Yeah. Right." She looked steadily at me. "You've got a nasty little gash above your left eye and quite a lump as well. Your face is a bloody mess." Pause. "Look, TC, there's a roadside park near St. Johns. Just up the road. We'll stop there and get you cleaned up. Why don't you go back and lay on the bed 'til we get there."

It was an idea I easily warmed to. The dog and I unsteadily changed places and once on the bed, I closed my eyes to ease the throb. Sleep snagged and dragged me away.

I awoke as I usually do, tumescent and tingled by some ill-remembered dream. Through one eye, I focused on Skilly's face as she dabbed, then dried my swollen-shut eye. Her face was soft, her breath sweet upon mine, her lips pursed in concentration. As she bent to me, the brilliant white of braless breasts peeked out through the top of her shirt.

Tumescence raged on. I laid there, oafishly shaking my head, awed speechless.

"So, I see you're up," she said, gazing into my open eye.

So I am, in more ways than one.

"Do you have a headache?"

It's a raging duet, if you must know.

"Want something to drink?"

Only the milk of human kindness, delivered through your breasts, and perhaps some labial nectar.

"Do you need a hand, TC?" accidentally (?) grazing my lap with her arm.

Oh, if only you knew...

Then, of all things, she kissed me. Not a peck, not a cheek brush, but full on my lips, full of promise. Dizzy with desire, I kissed back.

"Well, why not?" she said, standing up and slowly unbuttoning her shirt.

The surreal images of our tryst are forever etched within me: her no-nonsense nakedness, the ease with which she helped me shed my jeans. Grinning, she unhurriedly offered her breasts to my face, then turned away and lowered her head into my lap. The oral effect was electrifying though fitfully brief. Squatting over me, then settling herself onto me with a fond lubricity I had never known, she began seeking a rhythm and soon found a pace. Half-blind, half-stoned,

wholly half-witted, I could only watch, entranced, as her face
contorted, she tossed her head back, and rode on to our photo
finish. *Le petite mort.* How right the French are.

How long we lay locked together I cannot guess,
though I clearly remember it was in silence, a silence broken
only by our steady breathing and the occasional drone of a car
passing by on the nearby highway. Scarcely a word passed
between us as we dressed. In the awkward, eerie quiet, I was
touched with an odd sadness. *Post coitum, omne animal triste
est?* Skilly, on the other hand, was all business: she returned
to the driver's seat, urged the dog to the bed and me to the
passenger seat, and put us back on the road. The thunderous
silence continued. Ten minutes outside of Lansing, she finally
spoke.

"TC, about back there. You know, um, the sex. It
was...it was just something I had to do, right then, right there.
I was taken by the mood of the moment." She tried a weak
smile. "Bet you're not like that, living just for the moment.
Most Virgos aren't."

"Guilty," I confessed, "but I can see the benefits for
change." I offered my own weak smile. "Imagine the
moments like that I might have missed."

Skilly laughed lustily. "Seriously, TC. *Carpe diem.*
Seize the moment. You just never know...."

It was after midnight when she pulled up in front of
Hack's house, turned off the headlights, then turned to me.

"Hope your head's gonna be OK, TC. I really feel bad
about it," she said, reaching over and gently gliding a cool
hand over my lumpy eye. "I know this probably sounds weird,
but if you need a ride back up north, be out on 27 Sunday

morning and I'll look for you. I'm hoping to leave Ann Arbor
at 8:30. Should put me through here around ten."

"Gonna stop near St. Johns again?" I asked hoarsely.
The quick grin on her face gave me an answer.

"Maybe. Hold on to that moment, TC," she said, still
grinning. She leaned to me and gave me a chaste kiss on the
cheek.

Tugging at my suitcase, I eased out the side-door and
slammed it shut. I stood on the sidewalk and watched as she
pulled away, tail lights fading, at last disappearing as she
rounded a corner and vanished into the night. The warm
twinge at the base of my skull rekindled, then reblazed,
replacing the throb over my eye.

"What the hell you gonna' do, stand there 'til the sun
comes up? Get your sorry ass in here!" Hack called from the
front door of his house.

I managed the sidewalk and the steps onto the porch.
Hack finally saw my face in the dim glow of the porch light.

"Tsk, tsk, tsk," he murmured, shaking his head slowly.
"Stop a fist? I told you to never lead with your nose. TC, you
look like a plate of hammered shit."

Over a couple of beers, I told him the story of my trip:
the package, the ring, the 'mist' deer, the sex.

"What you won't go through to get laid, TC. Tell you
what, you won't have to mutilate yourself to score with these
State girls." Hack gulped down a swig of his beer. "Seriously
though, what do you suppose she's delivering?"

"Beats the hell out of me," was all I could answer.

Saturday dawned brightly beautiful, the autumn sun
promising a cloudless blue-sky day. Hack and I spent the

35

morning laying in supplies for the post-game party: a pony of beer, ice for the beer tub, a six-pack of Charmin ("Chicks drinkin' beer go through a lot of tp, TC."). Around noon, Hack's fianceé stopped in to tidy up the kitchen and bathroom ("Men are such pigs in a john," she observed.) A criminal justice major, Tina was petite, bubbly and beguiling, the antitheses of any cop I had ever encountered. She also looked distantly familiar.

"Oh, I know all about you," she said cop-like. "You once dated my kooky cousin Jenni Howard." She lowered her voice. "Well, what number were you, anyway?" she asked with a light, lilting laugh.

"Twenty three," I answered morosely, momentarily wondering if bed-notching was a familial trait.

"Last I heard, she was at 38 and counting. Surprised she's never gotten pregnant. Careless twit gives whoring a bad name," Tina chuckled, then erupted into a contagious laugh. Infected, I laughed, too.

As Tina tidied, I helped Hack ice-down the beer, then unscrambled a couple of Euchre decks. Party-ready, Hack and I drove to the stadium, leaving Tina to finish up. She had to work at the sheriff's office as part of her co-op program and couldn't make the game. She promised to be at the party later, promising also to bring along a date for me.

The football game was only mildly disappointing. The Spartans lost, but the game was close and unforgettably spirited. Seated in the State student section - a sea of green and white, awash with the rabidly raucous - I basked in the sun and the cool October wind, and thought about Skilly: the mystery of her mission, her live-for-the-moment mantra. I was rewarded with a now-familiar twinge.

Hack's party turned out to be an awesome showcase of Spartan spawn: the frat boys, the fat boys, the females, the fringe. Besotted with beer -- my face sunburned, windwhipped, cycloptic -- I watched, amused and amazed, as a steady stream of seasoned party-goers practiced the MSU hit-and-run: hit the beer, hit the Euchre game, hit the john, hit the road. By ten o'clock, only a dozen dogged drinkers remained, including Hack, Tina, me and my date, Janet, a strikingly pretty blue-eyed redhead. Sadly, we never hit it off. She seemed annoyed with my beery demeanor, I, with her "prettier than thou" detachment. Needless to say, I went to bed alone.

Sunday morning, Hack drove me to 27 North, just outside Lansing. As he dropped me off, he offered a bit of advice. "If you keep it in your drawers, TC, she may try to brain you again. I say whip out your love muscle the minute she stops to pick you up. That way, she won't have to cuff you to stuff you!"

I sat on my suitcase for three hours, waiting, watching the road, wondering. I turned down two rides, hoping she was simply running late. At one o'clock I gave in to the third offer, a *Free Press* feature writer heading up to Leland to research a piece about the lighthouses of the northern Lakes. He drove me all the way to Empire, right to my front door.

The phone call came late that Sunday night.

"Hello?"

"You OK?" Hack asked too quickly.

"Yeah, sure. Why?" I replied.

"You sitting down, TC?"

"C'mon Hack. What gives?" I snapped, irritation clipping my words.

"Your Volkswagen Virgo...she's dead, TC. It's all over the news down here."

"What?" I know I shouted.

"Got to be her, TC. She had an SDS ring on her finger."

"What happened?"

"Hit an 18 wheeler head-on near Ann Arbor Saturday night. Truck driver thinks she swerved to miss a deer or a big dog - he's not sure. She lost control, crossed the center line, and he pasted her. Driver's side of the freaking bus exploded on impact. Killed her and her dog instantly."

"Oh my God..."

"That's not the half of it. Cops discovered the chick was hauling around some kind of plastic explosive. Geologists use the stuff for mapping underground rock formations. You know, looking for oil deposits. Anyway, a deputy sheriff found a couple of unexploded packages under the passenger seat."

An uneasy chill clutched me, swept over me.

"And check this out. Tina heard on the sheriff's scanner that the State cops and the FB-freaking-I are looking for three guys. Something about an old guard SDS conspiracy to bomb college administration buildings next month. Apparently the girl was involved."

Of course she was, I said to myself.

"Hack, do you know the names of the guys involved?" I asked, hatching a hunch.

"Yeah. Some freaker here at State. Lennie the Red. Tina thinks they caught him already. Then there's some guy in Ann Arbor named Frederich. The other one's..."

"Named Karl, I'll bet," I said quickly.

"You got it, TC. Karl somebody from Mt. Pleasant."

Had to be, I thought. Couldn't be anyone else.

After hanging up the phone, I sat in my darkened room, embraced by the blackness and quiet. A spectral presence seemed to surround me, then seep into me. For only a moment it was there, a vision, twinging warmly at the base of my skull. The next moment it vanished.

Voices of Michigan

Doing Time

Erin Anderson

T hursday was book day. It had been that way ever since the old librarian had stopped coming around with the mobile library each day at three o'clock, ever since the jail had been reduced to three inmates and the old librarian had died of a heart attack. Now the Sheriff brought the books around himself without the pushcart. He just went to the library and picked up books, if anyone wanted one. All the inmates had been given Xeroxed copies of the local library's card catalogue listings. They had the entire week to peruse the list until Thursday when the Sheriff took their book orders. It was Thursday.

> **Erin Anderson** never realized the significance of her life in Michigan until she had lived away from home for a few years. It is only now, immersed in New York City, that her writing has begun to evolve from what she absorbed over 18 years spent in her Michigan home.

Munro had been allowed a razor against the standard incarceration policy. He had grown up next door to the Sheriff. He enjoyed several things that other inmates could not. Another was a mirror. Using these two items he shaved carefully each morning with nearly boiling hot water and no shaving soap. Thursday morning he stood in front of his mirror smoothly sliding the razor over the angular points of his face. He was not watching his reflection or thinking about his movements. He did not cut himself. Munro thought about

41

the book he had asked to be brought today. It was a travel guide, thick and square with a smooth plastic finish over the paperback cover. It was a travel guide to Antigua. He could see the word hovering in the air in front of him, taking the place of his forehead in the mirror's reflection. Antigua. He enjoyed the fact that the *gua* sounded like *gwa* and he could pronounce it correctly the first time he tried without anyone having to correct him. He tried to imagine the photograph on the cover. His eyes quickly became bubbling pools of electric blue water, his mouth a dune of dusty golden sand.

Over the sixty-two weeks Munro had been in jail he had read one book each week. That was their limit. Once a county social worker had visited the jail and asked him questions about what he was reading, why, and if he was enjoying it. She had written something on a stained legal pad and quickly gone away. That was when he was still reading novels, mainly horror and what the social worker had called "eroticism." He had started reading the travel guides about four months ago. He had first requested a book on Mexico because he knew someone from Mexico who had gone back home. He thought about him often and used to wonder what it was like there. At night he would lie in bed dreaming of the heat, trying to match Paulo's descriptions with his own world. In the morning he woke sleepy, his mind still thick with the textures of sun and sand.

Another privilege Munro enjoyed was the weekly visits from Loraine. She was allowed to visit Thursday afternoons from four to five o'clock. He looked forward to her coming nearly all week, except, when she finally came, he always felt preoccupied and slightly annoyed. She came too soon after his new book arrived, before he had time to look over the entire thing. Usually, though, he appreciated her company. She had long ago stopped wearing panties on her visits and often she would slide her chair flush with the entrance of his cell, her legs braced wide apart on the bars. When the Sheriff was not looking, he would kneel on the other side of the metal and duck his head beneath the folds of her skirt just to taste her on his tongue again.

Technically, Munro could not be held in jail before his trial, but he did not know that. The lawyer that had been appointed for him had not mentioned it either. He and the Sheriff were good friends. The Sheriff liked having someone in his jail to "look after."

"Book's here," the Sheriff called from the doorway. He walked in, his boots loud on the concrete floor, and tossed the book onto the bench under Munro's window. He turned, stopped, turned back and bent down again over the bench, narrowing his eyes at the cover. "Another travel book," he said, turning to go. "I think you're turning into my mother. She loves those things. Can't get enough of them." He smiled.

"You still live with your mother?" Munro asked, although he knew that he did.

"Yeah, I do. I take care of her. She couldn't get along without me," the Sheriff laughed, "that's what she always says." He had large square teeth which shone in the light. When he laughed he had the habit of raising his hands to his face and cramming the tips of his fingers into his mouth.

Munro hurried toward the bench and sat down with his book. The Sheriff left, the door ringing hollowly as it locked, chiming metal against metal. Munro studied the cover, felt the silky surface beneath his palm. The word

Antigua was written in simple white type on a light blue background. Above this block of blue there was a picture of a beach, the Antiguan beach, with white sand, nearly flourescent water, and a deep navy sky layered with full, curvaceous clouds. On the beach, the side of a thatch-roofed hut could be seen, its sides baked white in the heat. From the top of the cover hung a fringe of green palm fronds. One or two people, that looked like bugs, floated far out in the sea. *Antigua.* Munro greedily opened the book and began to read.

Munro heard a sharp cough and looked up. Lorraine stood in the door to his cell, her fingers fumbling with the zipper of her purse. Her eyes rested somewhere halfway between his own and the floor. It was four o'clock on a Thursday afternoon.

"Hey," he said. He set his book gently on the bench and stood up.

"Hi." She looked up slowly. He noticed the whites of her eyes were slightly discolored. They glistened in the reflection of the flourescent hallway lights, wet, as if they had been steeped in dirty water.

"Have a seat." Munro nodded toward a rusted metal folding chair outside the cell door.

"Thanks," she said softly. She always said that. *Thanks.* Munro found that funny, the timid way she waited for him to invite her to sit, like they were real people in a real house.

"So what's new?" he asked, trying to smile. He had been in the middle of a chapter on the outlying islands when she arrived.

"Nothing." She sighed and crossed her arms over her chest. He studied the dark, downy hair on her arms. She

44

rubbed her hands back and forth over them as if she were cold. The hair made a slight scratching sound like rubbing coarse wool. "I heard two guys talking about you outside," she said quickly, as if she were trying to push the words out of her mouth.

"Really?" he asked. Munro walked to the far side of the room, picked up his bench and dragged it across the concrete to the door. He sat down directly opposite Loraine. "So what were they saying?"

"Nothing really. One of them just wanted to know what you was in for."

"And what did the other one say? Who were they?" Munro asked, trying hard to seem interested. His eyes wandered briefly over his book, now resting on the floor under the window.

"I don't know. One of them was Tek. The other one, I don't know. Some kid, it looked like."

"What did he tell him?"

"He said arson." Loraine looked down at her shoes. She was wearing blue plastic pumps. She tried to squeeze the pointed toe in between the metal bars. "But it didn't sound like he believed you really did it or anything. Just that you burned the house. Not like it was on purpose to kill anybody," she finished softly and looked up.

"Oh. Good thing I didn't."

"Didn't what?"

"Kill anybody. That's in my favor. We just lost an old building they were going to tear down anyway."

"Yeah." Loraine looked blankly at Munro's chest.

He examined her face. Her gray eyes set closely toward the bridge of her nose made it appear clumsy and

45

disproportionately large. Her full lips were very red. He had always imagined those lips when he had read descriptions of the girl's faces in the novels he used to read. Her chin was small, almost nonexistent, with a large dimple in the center. Around her long neck she wore a pale blue scarf. *Antigua.*

"I've got to go," Munro said suddenly, standing up.

"Where is there to go?" Loraine asked, her thick lips drawing outwards into a smile.

Munro paused for a moment. "To the toilet. I've got to go to the toilet. I'll see you next week." He leaned quickly toward Loraine, pursing his lips and pushing them outward, as far from the rest of his face as possible. His lips reached hers with such taut forcefulness that they seemed to bounce back from each other as though they were made of thick elastic bands.

"I'll tell the Sheriff on the way out," she said quietly, looking down, watching her blue pumps carry her over the concrete to the office at the front.

"Thanks," he shouted after her, already on the way back to his book.

That night Munro did not sleep well. He moved fitfully on his thin mattress, the springs squeaking with the sound of old, angry metal. He dreamt of blues and bone-bleached whites, of heat and the sound of words like *Barbuda* and *Redonda*.

At first Munro had read only guides to the countries he felt had the most in common with his. He quickly devoured books on Norway, Scotland, France, Sweden, and the Netherlands. He especially enjoyed the book about England. It was the thickest guide they had and he often held it between his two palms, as if trying to gauge its weight, its worth, by its width. At times it seemed so thick, so juicy, with such a succulent cover, he felt he had to resist the urge to bite it through. There was one page Munro turned to the most in this guide. This page showed the outside of a modern-looking church, plain, and rather homely in contrast to the quaint London landscape. The face of the brick building was adorned with a rusted metal figurine of what looked like a calm and judicial Greek god. Underneath the sculpture were the words, "Not knowing sect or class, race or creed, each one is welcome in the service of all." Munro felt a sharp chill run fast through his body whenever he read these lines. He often imagined himself joining that congregation of worshipers, surrounded by what he imagined must be a perfectly diverse group of men and women of all sects, races, creeds, and classes. Many times he felt he was about to cry as he fancied he saw himself standing in a tightly-packed pew singing loudly an ardent hymn, his voice blending with the other worshippers in the "service of all." He felt proud of himself as he gazed upon his good deed. He felt proud that he was such a good person.

After he had exhausted his choices of countries reminding him of home, Munro moved east, toward what he considered the mysterious edge of Europe. The covers of these books displayed deeply colored cathedral murals, the sorcerer-like saints painted in dark reds, yellows, and gleaming whites, the colors of the body. Others exhibited cryptic moldings of ancient twisted metal, the pieces intertwined in a sacred golden weave. Here was something primeval and mystic, something pagan, he thought. Munro marveled that this fantastic world was real; that Hungary, Tuscany, the Ukraine, and Romania inhaled the earth's air, pulsated beneath the weight of their people and exhaled their crumbling vitality back into the atmosphere.

When summer came, the heat only fed Munro's craving for the scalding, the sweltering. As the summer wore on, he asked only for books about countries he envisioned as moist and hot, the damp radiating upwards in dripping clouds of steam. He wanted heat that was different from his own, heat that was purifying, heat that entered the body and ran out again from the pores, taking all impure things with it. The heat that he knew was dry and weak. There was no intensity to a Michigan summer. He was uncomfortable in his cell, but mainly this was from the stillness of the air, not the temperature. If the heat was moving somewhere, was rising and clinging to bulging droplets of moisture, at least that was something. At least it was alive.

For the remainder of the summer Munro continued to read about what he considered hot and therefore exotic climates. He requested books on Hawaii, Israel, Guatemala, Trinidad, Malaysia, Tobago, Barbados, and St. Lucia. During the week he was reading a guide to Bali and Lombok, he could not remove the image of these countries from his mind. Each night he would lie down to sleep already dreaming of lush green tiers of farmland overhung by fragrant palms. He read the sentence, "A jewel in the Indonesian archipelago," over and over in his mind until he felt he could sing himself to sleep with the music of it. *Archipelago.* He ate the sound of this word, held it in his mouth till he could no longer breath, then swallowed it whole.

Loraine's visits had grown shorter and shorter until one week she did not come at all. Munro had barely noticed. He was reading.

48

The Sheriff noticed. "Your girl must be sick this week," he said, smiling tensely, resisting the upward pull of his lips.

"Yeah," Munro nodded, not looking up from his book.

"It's funny though, I see her out a lot."

"Really." Munro still did not look up.

"Yeah," he said, beginning to laugh, "she gets out okay." The Sheriff walked away, jamming his fingers greedily between his brilliant teeth. Munro was only half-listening. His mind was filled, crowded with the sounds of his dreams, with the repetitive rhythm of unfamiliar worlds, cities and nations: *Lisbon, Nigeria, South Africa, Bulgaria*

The next week on Thursday at four o'clock, Loraine was there. She wore a short denim skirt with a red, ribbed tank top. There were plastic thongs on her feet.

"Hi there," said Munro, sitting on his bench opposite her.

She moved her chair to its familiar position against the bars. "Hi."

He waited for her to continue, to start something. He could not think of anything to say.

"Sorry about last week," she said finally. Her words were rushed, muffled in their hurry.

"It's all right," Munro answered calmly, his face blank and unimpressed.

"I made plans and I just forgot until it was too late and it was way past five o'clock," she focused her eyes on his for an instant, then quickly looked away.

"That's fine," Munro said. "What were your plans?" He turned to look out his window. He thought he had heard thunder in the distance. Outside, a car squealed suddenly on the asphalt.

"Oh, I just went out. With some friends," Loraine looked up quickly then back down at her dirty yellow thongs. "Olson was there. He brought a cousin of his. He's an architect," she let the end of her sentence linger in the air until the last syllable was exhausted. She sat silently, her eyes on Munro's face.

He sat up quickly on the bench. "What kind of architect?" he asked abruptly.

Loraine's bushy eyebrows wrinkled in surprise. She moved back slightly in her chair. "What do you mean?"

"What kind of architect is he? What does he build?"

"He doesn't build. He just designs, I think." Loraine turned her head and looked quickly behind her toward the office and then back at Munro with a narrow sideways glance. "Office buildings or something."

Munro sat back on the bench. *Intriguing Creole architecture.* "Did you have a good time?" *St. Lucia.* Munro sighed and ran his fingers over the bridge of his nose. *Stunning and eccentric cityscape.* He lowered his eyes as Loraine sat back in her chair, her legs slightly apart. *Lisbon.*

"Sure. It was all right." She shifted in her chair. The metal leg scraped across the concrete floor.

Munro noticed she was starting to spread her legs. He leaned forward on the bench, placing his forehead against the bars, and looked down the hall toward the office. The hallway was empty. A tired fan oscillated back and forth on the table. As she lifted her thonged feet onto the walls of his cell, he could see the obscure black expanse between her legs giving way to the positive definition of flesh, leg, inner thigh, and pubic hair. He watched as a dark spot, the size of a fist,

50

emerged on the inside of her leg, just below her carelessly shaved bikini line. It spread across her thigh like a running bruise, fresh and barefaced.

"What is that?" Munro said much too loudly, jerking back quickly on the bench.

"Be quiet," Loraine said in a grating whisper. Her legs remained parted on the bars, a pink diamond sparkling between them. "It's a sun," she answered.

Munro leaned forward, his elbows on his knees. He squinted and turned his head sideways. He did not recognize her. As he moved closer, Loraine moved toward him until she was touching the dark metal. She shivered as it made contact with her skin. Her head fell slightly back and her eyelids lowered partially.

She waited.

The sun was the color of thick flesh, weathered and sagging, and outlined in a wet-rock blue. The rays encircling the yellow disk were serpentine waves, curving in and out of the landscape of skin. They sprawled there in wait, so many arachnid legs frozen motionless by the parting of her thighs.

Munro got up suddenly. The wood of the bench squealed against the worn floor. He walked to the window and looked out at the cars parked under the shade of a wilting elm. The drive leading to the jail was all dirt, hard packed, with no gravel. Now, in the heat, the dust rose so thick with a passing car that, for a moment, it blotted out the sun. It was the county's doctor, moving slowly in the shadow of the risen cloud, for his monthly visit to check Munro's heart, pulse and reflexes: to make sure he was still breathing.

"Well?" Loraine said, her eyes wide and her eyebrows raised.

Munro said nothing.

Lisbon, Nigeria, South Africa, Bulgaria.

Loraine did not come back.

The next week Munro requested a guide to Belize. He felt it must be a mixture of both island other-worldlyness and ancient stability with its roots in the very core of the earth.

His trial was to be held in Grand Rapids, some ninety miles away. The lawyer had come frequently in the past few weeks to discuss procedural matters with Munro and answer his questions. He did not have any questions. Sometimes the Lawyer would stay and talk with the Sheriff after talking to Munro. He was blond-haired with his face shaved extremely close and wore a great amount of very strong after-shave. Munro guessed he was probably twenty-five years old.

Thursday his guide to Belize arrived and the lawyer came. Even after the lawyer had explained the next week's trial and what Munro was to say, and gone to talk with the Sheriff, he could not read. He watched them talk in the open, back doorway, the Sheriff routinely feeding his fingers between his teeth and sucking greedily. Munro would wait until they had gone to pick up his book which lay untouched on the bench.

Outside his window a migrant family methodically picked cherries from the young trees which bordered the jail. He remembered summers years ago when thousands of workers arrived in late July to spend the next month harvesting the dark fruit from the trees. It had been his favorite time of the year. Sometimes he would lie in the orchard grass for hours, feeling the sharp, cool blades graze his skin. Then the machines came to gather the fruit and the workers disappeared, only remaining in the few orchards with trees too small to shake.

A thin woman with strong, dark arms was calling her three children to eat. Two small boys and an unusually tall girl came to meet her underneath the sugar maple which grew against the east wall of the jail. Her husband was already there, lying with his arms folded underneath his head, staring up through the branches. She began pulling food from a blue plastic cooler and handing it out to the children. They ate silently, rubbing their noses often with red sticky hands. The woman began talking to her husband. Munro could not understand their words. She shook him by the shoulder until he rolled onto his side and propped his head up with his elbow. He listened intently. She gestured frequently, many times beating his knee with the flat palm of her hand for emphasis. Sometimes she would look over her shoulder at the children rolling around in the grass. The two boys were spitting cherry pits at the tall girl. The woman spoke sharply to the boys and, yet, it seemed she continued to speak to her husband, her sentences moving in an unbreakable rhythm which moved forward and back, rolling smoothly over and under themselves.

Munro watched the family until long after the lawyer had gone and the Sheriff had returned to his office. Once the sun had moved west, no longer burning intently from overhead they collected their things and moved back to the orchard. As they rose to leave, Munro felt a strange tearing in the bottom of his stomach and he was surprised to find himself still standing on the concrete of his cell, still himself, separate from them. For those few moments, he had become so involved in listening to their speech and in watching their faces and movements that he had forgotten he was an individual with set boundaries between self and not self. He had felt the infinite possibilities of otherness. How is it I am not they, Munro asked himself. How is it I can look at that woman, at that hair, that skin, those fingernails stained red with juice and not live within them, not be a part of them? How is it I am here and they were able to walk away?

The trial was held on a Thursday. Book day. Because of the long drive in the van and the guaranteed wait at the courthouse, Munro was allowed to keep his book on Belize past the due date and take it with him to his court appointment.

Munro, the Sheriff, and someone who the Sheriff called "my guard," but whom Munro had never seen before, left the jail at six o'clock Thursday morning. Munro did not read during the car ride. Instead, he sat in the seat beside the large, side window and watched the blue dawn turn light, his book clutched so tightly in his hands it became slippery to the touch. He could not bring himself to read yet. He wanted to save it for later, when he would need it. All he could do was stare at the cover, at the different shades of blue in which the ruins of an ancient temple were photographed. It was nighttime in the picture and a full moon with blue clouds hung on the edges could be seen at the left of the crumbling rotunda of the old observation tower. Two small windows were visible in what remained of the rounded top. He imagined himself climbing the circular staircase, his steps rich and echoing, to the top of the rotunda. Perhaps they were very much like the steps displayed on the cover, wide and long, as long as two normal steps put together, with lines intersecting them at regular intervals to show where the stone blocks were laid together. He envisioned himself standing at one of those windows, his forearms grating on the rough stone sills and looking out at that moon. He tried to think of what might be on the other side of the temple. More steps like those shown? An ocean, a cliff? He could not decide and realized he did not want to know. It would be too much to take in, too much to absorb, and he was glad for the security of the two-dimensional photograph which kept the possibilities of experience in the realm of the understandable. Whatever it was, he knew it would be blue, like everything else in that world, blue like Belize. Blue. It was a blue different from anything he had ever seen, varying in its appearance from object to object. But never could he believe it was not the same blue. Only the objects transformed it, acted upon it. It was a blue of deep night sky and early dawn, of soft wet grasses, and sad stone. He knew that if he were to walk into that blue it would color him too, until it replaced everything inside him. If he were to fall on the edge of a jagged stone, his blood would run blue over the cragged surface like water.

The courtroom was on the tenth floor of a gray rectangular building with shining metal window frames and smoky, tinted glass. Munro did as he was told. He stood, walked, sat, and talked when someone asked him to. Finally, he was allowed take his seat on a black padded chair behind a long wooden table. The table looked as if it had been polished that morning. His fingers felt oily after touching it. On his way to the front of the room, he passed Loraine sitting on a bench a few rows behind his long oak table. She was wearing a denim dress he had never seen before and wore her hair up and pinned in a knot at the back of her head. For seem reason he looked at her feet and noticed she still wore her yellow thongs, which she had tried to hide by keeping her feet under the pew. Munro knew she owned other shoes and thought it strange. He sat down next to his lawyer who looked as if he had been waiting a long time and was annoyed. He shook Munro's hand and smiled widely, displaying his very red gums. He said something and Munro nodded his head, then he patted Munro roughly on the back before turning back to his papers. He was wearing even more after-shave than usual.

As soon as someone began talking in the courtroom, it began to rain. It rained hard the whole day. Munro leaned toward the window beside his chair and looked down at the sidewalk, lined with perfectly placed green shrubs, below. Everything was wet. If he looked straight out the window, at eye level, his view was above the trees, and still the rain was only passing through this section of sky, on its way further down from somewhere further up. He felt surprised somehow that rain began so high in the air, so far from people, and not lower, at a place just above their heads.

Munro listened disinterested as another lawyer, older and wearing suspenders, and several witnesses described his actions on a night several months before. He heard them explain how he left a bar after fighting with one of his old high school classmates. He heard different witnesses give different reasons for why they were fighting. He heard them recount how he had staggered from the bar home to his garage, taken his acetylene torch and some oily rags from his workbench and walked to the man's house, where he threw a rock wrapped in burning oily rags through the front window, and watched as their home burned, only rushing to their door at the last minute and hollering up the stairs to wake everyone and help pull the children from the arms of their struggling parents.

Munro did not remember. He did not know if they were telling the truth, but he realized that they might be. All he knew was that he had not killed anyone, that no one had died. He could not understand why they continued to talk. People were alive. He felt that was all that should matter. When he was brought to the witness stand, he answered everyone's questions quickly and directly, his eyes focused intently on the floor in front of him or out the window at the rain.

He was relieved when he was finally allowed to return to his seat and his book. He left it lying still on the table, centered perfectly in front of him. He rested his elbows on the table and placed his fingertips lightly on the soft cover. *Belize.*

Munro watched as Loraine was called to the witness stand. He noticed how short her skirt was and that her heels were dirty. She sat in the chair next to the Judge's bench and looked serious, as though she were concentrating very hard. Strands of her light brown hair kept escaping from the loose rubber band at the back of her head and falling in front of her eyes. She tried to smooth them back into place with quick furious movements. Munro saw that her hands were shaking.

Loraine was now saying something about Munro. That he was a good man, most of the time, and he only had a bad temper when he was drinking. She was saying she was quite sure that he had done nothing wrong that night and had come straight to her house after he left the bar. The lawyer with the suspenders looked quickly to the jury and then back at Loraine. He began talking about the word "quite." Loraine looked scared.

It was beginning to get dark outside. An evening moon shone palely over the branches Munro could see from his seat. He looked at the moon on the cover of his book, its texture rich and light. He was sure he knew what it felt like to stand beneath that moon, to feel its cool rays on his skin. He was positive he knew everything there, the way no one else ever could. He knew the way the third step from the top dipped down in a slight depression and that it was here that one could sit for hours overlooking everything below the ruins. Munro could not understand how it was that this place, this world he knew so intimately, could not be a part of him, how it was that he was separated from it by the table, the cover, the air. He had been everywhere, traveled everywhere and, yet retained nothing. All the places he had been he was not allowed to keep. They had been diffused into words and come back together in two-dimensional portraits, of which, when he studied them, he had but a dim recollection. And it was this vague remembrance which inspired in him such a deep nostalgia that he was nearly drowned at times with the longing to go home. He remembered the migrant family picking cherries, their smiles, their skin, their laughter. He remembered everything about their lives in those brief moments, as if he had lived their entirety, had been inside them, had been them, each one of them. He felt pieces of his brain had been picked from beneath his skull and set down in the bodies of separate entities who were then wound up and set off to walk along their separate lives. "That was me," Munro thought. Now those things, those lives and places of energy were free, and he was alone, not quite together anymore, not quite himself. "I was once a whole person."

The lawyer with the suspenders continued to talk, his eyes boring into Loraine who had slumped forward on the witness stand, her head resting on her crossed arms. The jury shifted uncomfortably as the lawyer's voice rose in pitch, his arms flailing wildly. He pointed often to Munro. Outside it was now blue-dark and the moon's light full, although defused by the fluorescent lighting inside the courtroom. Munro turned to the window. *Belize.* His lawyer leaned toward him, cupping his hand around Munro's ear, he lowered his voice. He said something about being "stuck" and their having to forget getting off entirely. The lawyer with the suspenders shouted to the jury, calling their attention to Munro's obvious callousness, his unfeeling nature, his inattention to the trial. Munro could only think about everything he had released from his body, everything that was separate from him, connected only by nostalgia. He thought of all he had lost in his life. The lawyer continued, reminding the jury of the cold-bloodedness it took to burn someone's family home to the ground. His lawyer turned to him as if to whisper again. Munro leaned in to say something and stopped. He was innocent. He had tried to save them at the last minute. The lawyer finished.

Suddenly there was a loud noise from the front of the courtroom. Munro turned to see Loraine topple forward, crumbling the way a wounded animal would fall. Her chair slid out from under her as her forehead hit the wooden banister surrounding the witness stand with a far-away hollow sound. He watched as several of the jurors rushed over from their box. The one in front, who reached Loraine first, had large tanned arms which bulged from the tightly rolled-back sleeves of his white dress shirt. He lifted Loraine up from the

floor in one swift movement and set her back in the tall
wooden chair. She had opened her eyes and was beginning to
regain consciousness. The courtroom was loud with circular
whirlwinds of chatter, despite the Judge's constant banging
with his gavel.

Munro continued with what he had wanted to say
before to his lawyer; not noticing the commotion, instead,
feeling within it all the space through which he had
wandered, all the room he had created for his various selves.
His voice, although contained behind his cupped hand,
echoed clear and loud in the humming courtroom, "At least
everyone got out," he said. "At least I let everyone out."

The Wreckage of the Savior

Noah Lein

The Discovery

The sonar pulsed rapidly. Jack Henson, Navy Captain in the Gulf of Mexico, gave orders to his crew, talking fluently without a pause.

"Visual," he said, and two technicians typed on keyboards until a green object appeared on the screen.

"What is it?" he asked. Henson always wanted answers, and he always wanted them now.

One of the men said, "A sunken ship is my guess. It's only one mile from the Florida coast, though."

"No," he said, biting his lip. "Ships fish around here all the time; cruise ships, cable layers, oil tankers, you name it. Someone must have picked it up. It's only two hundred feet down. A cheap, ten-dollar, fish-finder could pick this up."

Another technician agreed, "You're right. But how do you explain the huge shipwreck down there?"

Henson almost laughed, "I'm not going down there. Get an inspection team."

"Any press?" somebody asked.

"Heck no, we're the Navy, for God's sake. We don't

> **Noah Lein** lives near Elk Rapids, Michigan. He has enjoyed writing longer books for the past ten years, but more recently began writing short stories. Noah is a sophomore in high school who enjoys writing, drumming, skiing, golf and basketball.

go preaching all of our discoveries to the press," Henson yelled. "I don't want them crawling around me for the next ten years. Let's keep this one quiet."

The Dive

The inspection team arrived only two hours later, ready to go. Henson's men suited them in underwater equipment with thirty minutes of air.

"Find the name, find the origin, and find out how it got here," were his instructions.

I didn't want to go down there. I had been involved on search dives before, but not with ships that appear out of nowhere.

The team consisted of Harry Adams, an oceanographer from Miami; Melissa Jacobs, a woman who had been diving all her life, and had trained for underwater exploration; Mary Olin, a marine biologist; and me. My name is Rick Harrison and I'm the leader of the team. I didn't go to college. I joined the Navy and was under Henson's command.

We dove in, and began the swim down. We had not gone down far when the masts and crow's nest of a ship appeared in the dark water. Through radios, Mary said, "It's beautiful."

Melissa and Mary began to 'ooh' and 'ah' at the ship until I shut them up by saying, "Let's get this over with quickly. Remember: find the name, and then we'll find the origin, and why it's here."

They all waved at me in agreement.

The whole boat came into view. It was massive. The deck was eighty to one hundred feet at least. Three masts would have supported its body back in its time, and the bowsprit shot forward like an arrow.

Before Melissa could restart her annoying admirations, I said, "Find a name plate, or a label of some kind."

We split into two groups, Melissa and I on one side and Mary and Harry on the other.

As we swam around its hull, I heard Harry whispering, "This gives me the creeps."

"What are you afraid of, Harry?" Mary asked.

I smiled behind my mask, shining my flashlight on the ship's side. "He's afraid that this thing is a haunted ghost ship." I happened to feel the same way.

"You two are just superstitious," Melissa commented. So far, no luck with our ship's name.

"You know what scares me a little?" Mary said. "This thing has no punctures, injury marks, not even a scratch. If this ship sunk, God must have picked her up and placed her down here."

"I doubt that," Melissa said.

"Don't have much faith in God now, do you, Melissa?" I asked.

"No, I just doubt that God would put this ship here for no obscene reason, that's why."

Mary snickered. "I hope these radio transmissions aren't on the record. Henson's going to be mad. We sound like idiots down here."

Then I saw it. On a huge plate, in fancy letters was:

S.S. Thomas Smith

"There's our name, guys. Let's go back to the surface after we meet in the front of the ship," I said.

Melissa and I paddled quickly. I took a waterproof camera out of my suit and snapped several photos of the name.

We met in the front. "Did you get pictures?" Mary asked.

"Ten Kodak's," I said, smiling.

The four of us were about to leave when Harry suddenly said, "I'm not feeling good."

"It's just the pressure, Harry. Let's go up."

Harry shook his head. "No. My head...I'm seeing spots...red."

Mary shook him and yelled, "Come on, Harry. You'll be fine at the top."

Then I saw the carbon dioxide meter on his suit. It was dangerously high.

"Oh, God," I yelled. "Get him up to the surface, now!"

Harry then passed out.

Melissa was screaming, "Hurry! Now!" and tugging at Harry's arms.

And then, as we tried to move him, his body was thrown into muscle spasms and his face glass shattered as it hit the body of the ship.

Harry was dead.

I couldn't believe it. A flaw in Harry's air circulation system had obviously caused the carbon dioxide to stay in his air tanks to the point where he breathed in the deadly gas.

Blood flowed freely from his gashed face.

"Let's take his body up," Mary said slowly, after almost two minutes of silence.

But we had waited too long. In the distance, I saw a

great white shark. It smelled the blood and that was what it wanted. If it caught us towing the body to the surface, we'd be dead, too.

"We have to leave him," I said. "Let's go."

"Are you nuts? We aren't going to leave him here at the bottom of the ocean!" Melissa screamed.

"We don't have time for this! Look behind you!"

Melissa looked. She was silent for a moment, and then nodded. We began our ascent to the surface.

As I was brought on board the Navy ship, I passed out.

The Life

I awoke two hours later in a hospital bed. Though I had only fainted, the Navy required that I be taken care of by a medical doctor because I had just come up from a dive. I sat up, moaning for water. The nurse went to bring me some, but I fell asleep while she was gone.

The next day was sunny, bright and beautiful. Just the opposite of how I felt. I looked at the beds beside me. There was an empty one and another with a patient on it who I thought was sleeping. I really couldn't tell because he had a huge patch on his face.

Henson was in the room, talking to Mary, who was drinking a mug of coffee, looking at the floor as she answered questions. Her bed was in a dark corner of the room, far from me.

Henson stopped with her and I knew I was next. Mary sighed and lay back down to sleep. He approached my bed.

"I'm sorry," he said. "Somehow Harry's tank was not built right, and..." he stopped.

I nodded slowly.

65

"Can you answer some questions?"

I sighed. "Can't a man wake up properly these days?"

"I have to, Harrison. Some things went on down there that need to be cleared up."

"Go ahead," I agreed.

"Okay. What was the ship's name?"

"The **S.S.** *Thomas Smith*."

"Okay," he said, writing on a pad of paper. "And how big was it?"

"I don't know. About a hundred feet long. Pretty big."

Henson nodded. "And why did you come back to the surface without Harry?"

I was confused. "What?"

"You understood me."

"Okay, because Harry's carbon dioxide level was dangerously high, he died from it, he went into a spasm, his face hit the ship, and there was blood everywhere. A shark smelled the blood and we had to ascend to the surface without him."

Henson shook his head at me. "That's what your partners said, also. Well, I think you should be happy to know that Harry is not dead, but in a coma."

I must have lost it at that point, "WHAT?"

"He's in the bed beside yours."

I gaped at the bed beside me. The man's face was covered where Harry's scars must be.

"A cargo ship found his body afloat in the Gulf. We saw them in the harbor and identified him as Harry Adams."

I was still in disbelief.

"The ship then sailed back out to the ocean. It was an

old one."

"No," I protested. "You don't understand. Harry passed out from carbon dioxide poisoning, then went into a spasm smashing his facemask and then his face. A shark got his remains. Harry is dead, sir."

"No, he's not, Harrison. He's right next to you." Henson walked away, disgusted.

I couldn't believe it. The man next to me may not be Harry. Maybe it's somebody else, I thought.

But those thoughts vanished as a nurse came in and took off the bandages, revealing Harry's battered face. She replaced the old ones with new ones. It was Harry.

Nobody discovered the ship's origin. Mary didn't know it at the time, but her little theory about God putting the ship there was true to me. Why? The next time divers investigated the ship, its name wasn't the **S.S. *Thomas Smith***, but...

S.S. *Harry Adams*

Voices of Michigan

Love Unending

Ann Snider

Dedicated to my parents who have inspired me to
achieve my dreams and
in loving memory of Emily Anderson and Katy Clemens
whose short lives touched us all.

I sat on my bed with my legs crossed, reviewing my past week. Tears trickled down my face. Silent tears in long, narrow rivers of pain that never seemed to end. Just a few short days ago everything had been fine. A few short days ago, I had been a normal sixteen-year-old girl with normal friends and a normal life. Well, as close as you can get to normal. Then my whole world fell apart. It's amazing how fast your entire life can change--change with no warning and you with it. Just a few days ago. . . .

Ann Snider was born on November 27, 1983. She began writing at an early age. It has been and still is for pleasure, but she has always dreamed of being published. She lives with her family and several pets in Michigan. This was a composition in eighth grade when Ann was 14.

"Hey Gabs, pass it here!" screamed Kevin over the din.

"Gabby, over here!" shouted Taylor.

"Gabs?" questioned Eric.

I flew by them all, both teams. My target locked, my goal in mind. Nothing was going to deter me from my mission.

The wind whipped through my black curly hair and stung my dark brown eyes. My blue and red jersey clung to my deeply tanned skin as I flew through the short grass. Two seconds left. A simple kick here at this angle........Whoo hoo goal! Right at the buzzer! Gabriella Rodreguez scores the winning goal in the last game of the tournament, resulting in the final score, 4-3.

Elated with my victory, I threw my arms in the air and whooped and cheered as my teammates and coach ran over to congratulate me. I quickly became the center of a human sandwich that squished me with the weight and bodies of seventeen teenage boys and a huge coach. I was so happy, I didn't care. I was floating, soaring high above the ground with pride. Okay, that's over doing it I thought to myself but suddenly I realized I was! I was floating above the ground on the shoulders of eighteen men! I was being carried off the field!

"Gabby!" I turned at the sound of my name. Looking behind me, I saw Alexis standing, beaming from ear to ear. She waved and game me a thumbs-up sign. We got to the spectators' side of the field and they put me down. Everyone went to find their families and friends. I ran to Alexis.

Alexis and I had been best friends since kindergarten. For eleven years! We had grown up together and knew everything about one another. She was the sister I never had; brother, too, for that matter. She was family.

We embraced in a hug and she held me at arms length. Studying me, she smiled. "My best friend--a sophomore--captain of the boys' soccer team--MVP for two years--a champion--a star," she said with awe and appreciation, and we hugged again. Over her shoulder, I saw a tall, dark, handsome guy approaching.

"Todd!" I cried. Alexis released me and I ran straight into the strong arms of the football team captain, the 4.0 junior, my boyfriend--Todd Regean.

"You did it!" he cried. "You led the team to a victory!"

"We did it," I corrected him as the team gathered around with their girlfriends. "We did it together."

I smiled as I viewed the scene. Taylor walked over and hugged Alexis.

"Let's celebrate?" he shouted. "Everyone up for Pizza Palace?" He was rewarded with an approving uproar from everyone.

"As long as the girls can come," replied Steve, "and Todd, of course."

I didn't mind. I was used to being one of the guys. I liked it that way. It had taken a while at first, but when the boys saw my abilities, they had come around.

"All right!" I shouted enthusiastically. "Come on everybody!" This started a mass stampede toward the parking lot. Todd, Taylor, Alexis and I took our time. Todd has his own car and so did Alexis. We knew we wouldn't be left without a ride.

"Can Alexis and I ride with you guys?" asked Taylor.

"I don't think I'm gonna go," replied Alexis touching her head lightly with her hand. "I don't feel that great. You guys go on and have fun. I'll see you Monday at school."

"Are you sure?" Todd asked. "I have plenty of room."

"Positive," she replied putting her small hand on Todd's arm. She smiled and playfully shooed us to the parking lot. "Now get going you two champions. You too

Todd. They are going to start the victory party without you!"

Taylor gave her a hug and a brief kiss. "I'll call you," he told her.

"Bye," I said, hugging her after the boys were in the car. "You call me," I teased.

"I will. Bye." She climbed into her car and I got into Todd's. Little did I know that that would be the last time I, or Taylor or anyone for that matter would hug her or walk with Alexis or hang out with her again.

"For she's a jolly good fellow--which nobody can deny!"

We were at Pizza Palace and the guys decided to humiliate me in front of the entire restaurant. With evil grins on their faces, they stood and sang For *She's a Jolly Good Fellow* for me just for laughs. Boy did it work. We had everyone in the joint splitting at the seams. When they were finished, they sat back down and I managed to steer the conversation away from the song and back to the game.

After two hours, fifteen pizzas, countless pitchers of pop, three burping contests (which I won all of, thank you) and two straw-wrapper fights, we decided to call it quits. Everyone was stuffed and the waitress had started to give us disgusted looks over our lingering and activities. With a final cheer and another round of *For She's a Jolly Good Fellow*, we all thanked our coach, said good-bye to each other and left.

Todd, Taylor and I all piled into Todd's car.

"That was fun!" exclaimed Taylor enthusiastically. "Too bad it has to end."

"Who says it does?" I replied. "We'll just move the party to my place with us and Alexis. My folks won't mind. We'll call her from my house."

"Okay," chorused the guys and off we went.

Todd eased his car into my driveway and parked it in his normal spot. We all got out and headed toward the house.

As I opened the door that led from the garage to the kitchen, I shut a chapter in my life. The end of the young girl who never wanted to grow up found that she must as she was about to face what was next. This event changed my life forever.

I saw my mom and dad on the couch together. Their backs were to us and they sat still.

"Hey Mom! Dad! We won! It was awesome! Taylor and Todd are here. Can we hang out here and call Alexis to come too?" I cried oblivious to the tension in the room.

My dad slowly turned around and my mom stood and walked toward me at a sluggish speed. Their faces were red and---tear stained? My parents were crying? That couldn't be? Then what was this foreign, unfamiliar substance on their face? It had to be tears.

"Mom?" I uttered, my voice low.

"Oh baby!" she cried. She broke into a gait, leaped the last few feet and threw her arms around me.

I was more confused than I had been in my life. My parents were crying---I had decided that indeed tears were running down their faces---and my mom was hugging me. She had stopped doing that long ago, at least in front of my friends.

"Baby," my mom sobbed in a whole new flood of tears. "I just got a call a half an hour ago. Alexis' car was hit by a truck. She is in the hospital. We were waiting for you to go there."

A darkness passed over my eyes and I fell backwards

73

but regained my balance just as Todd steadied me. I shook my head and the darkness cleared. Behind me I could hear Taylor's muffled sob. I heard every car that went by and every bird in the trees. I smelt things in my house I no longer noticed, like the smell of our carpet cleaner, long since used. My senses became so acute and I sucked up every detail. At the same time, my head was reeling. No, this couldn't be happening. No. This happens on bad soap operas but not to normal, good families like ours.

"Let's go," I muttered. "I want to ride with Todd and Taylor," I said, "if Todd'll take me." I looked at him and saw a tear trickle down his cheek. He wiped it away hastily, obviously embarrassed.

"Of course I will," he said taking my hand. "Let's go." He guided me toward the car and I was grateful. I couldn't see very well and my balance was completely gone. I was glad for a strong arm to hold me up.

It was quiet all the way to the hospital except for an occasional sob from the worried Taylor in the back seat. Todd was concentrating on the road, and he held my hand reassuringly. All these thoughts were running through my head. Feelings I couldn't describe or even put my finger on. Memories of everything we'd done together came flooding back. I didn't cry because I knew she couldn't die. There was no way God could take my best friend. This couldn't happen to me. Not to my friend. Not to Alexis.

We pulled into the hospital with my parents right behind us. We walked into the entrance and the horrible smell of sickness and death filled my nose and lungs.

After checking with the front desk, we walked down the long hall to room 418. When we walked into her room and I saw her laying there--so pale and still, I broke down. Reality hit me and I realized she could die. She looked bad enough. She had tubes coming out of her from everywhere. Her flawless skin was covered in cuts and bruises, masking her beauty.

My parents and Alexis' parents left to go talk and to leave the four of us alone.

Todd enfolded me in a hug and Taylor went to the bedside. He knelt down beside her and buried his face in his hands which held hers. After several minutes, he stepped back. Todd let me go and went to Taylor. He patted him on the back and started to try to console him in a hushed voice. I went and pulled up a chair by Alexis' bed. I smoothed her soft brown hair away from her face. I took her clammy hand and in a steady voice and with a dry face, I began talking to her. It didn't matter to me that she was unconscious. I knew she needed to hear my voice. I told her about the party at Pizza Palace and reminded her of some of our fun times together.

I had just gotten to the part where we made ourselves sick on a ride at an amusement park when I heard a faint voice whisper my name. Surprised, I looked down at Alexis and saw her smile.

"Gabby," she said weakly as she gently squeezed my hand.

"Yes," I replied anxiously. The boys gathered behind my chair, as excited as I was.

"Gabby, I love you," she said.

"No!" I shouted. "No, Alex. You are not saying good-bye to me! You are going to be fine! You are going to live!"

"Gabs, please," she pleaded and one look at her sad

eyes made me stop. She needed me to understand and be with her, not scold her.

"You are my best friend and my blood sister," she continued and I smiled, remembering the time when we were eight and became blood sisters by the lake. "Tell my parents I love them. Is Taylor here?" she asked.

Taylor jumped forward to Alexis' side. "I'm here Alex," he said softly.

"I love you," she said. "Never forget that."

"Oh Alex," he sobbed and broke down. "I love you too."

"Don't cry," she begged gently with a sad smile. Todd took Taylor's shoulders and pulled him behind my chair. Alexis' breathing became labored and she looked at me and smiled weakly again.

"I love you," she whispered. Her eyes closed, the beautiful blue eyes that always held a twinkle in them had closed for the last time. She lay completely still as I laid my head down on the hands that held her lifeless ones and cried. I knew my best friend was gone and there was nothing that could be done. I felt as if my heart had been ripped out and my soul with it. Somewhere behind me, I felt Todd put his hand on my shoulder and the door open, bringing along with it my parents' voices as well as the voices of Alexis' parents. I heard Alexis' mom begin to cry inconsolably and her dad begin to try to comfort her. I heard Todd cry without shame, and my parents as well, but none of this mattered. Alexis was gone. She was gone. . . .

Tears trickled down my face from the renewed pain. 0They jolted me back to the present. Remembering the funeral and the casket being lowered into the ground---how horrible it had all been. My life would never be the same I remember thinking at the cemetery. Never.

I unfolded my legs and stood up. I put on my shoes and grabbed my jacket. I had decided to go to Todd's house to talk with him. I was starting to heal and though I knew it would be long and hard, I knew I could do it.

On my way, I stopped by the cemetery. Kneeling by the freshly dug grave, I placed a bouquet of flowers down. Stroking the dirt gingerly, I whispered the last words she had said to me, "I love you."

Voices of Michigan

Remembrances

Laura Robinson

[handwritten inscription: To Dave and Marilyn, Laura]

The funeral was held, appropriately, on a gray, drizzling day in mid-October. It was a typical funeral in most respects: the family was seated in the front, the casket was open, and the sounds of muffled sobs carried softly through the gathering of mourners. It was not a difficult funeral to attend; the deceased had lived a long and vibrant life, had outlived all of her siblings and her husband, and most of those present were acquaintances of her children. Her eldest spoke of her loves and her life, the pastor spoke of her redemption and her place in heaven, and her favorite hymns were sung. Finally, the young men selected to be pallbearers carried the casket out the door and into the waiting hearse.

> **Laura Robinson** was born and raised in Battle Creek, Michigan. She is the stay-at-home mother of two daughters and one son. Along with being an avid reader, she is also interested in tatting, embroidery, and all types of crafts. She and her husband, Ron, reside in Amelia, Ohio.

After the graveside service and the dinner presented by the graying members of the Women's Guild at the church, he paid his respects to the family, tears still stinging at his wrinkled, red eyes, made his way to his rental car and drove off.

"Dad, who was that man?" asked her eldest grandson.

"I don't know. I wondered that myself."

He drove back to Kalamazoo and returned the rental

car. He presented his boarding pass and shuffled aboard the airplane. He knew he looked like hell, but he didn't care. It was finally over. His hopes, dreams, ended when the top of that casket was closed. She really hadn't changed that much in 53 years. She was still the most beautiful woman he had ever seen in his life. He found his seat, leaned back and closed his eyes, exhausted.

He had thought he would be the next Glenn Miller or Tommy Dorsey. He smiled, remembering how cocky he had been when he had first seen her. She had come down the stairs at her family home, interrupting him while he was playing his sax for her brother. He had wanted so badly to be in their band, and had persuaded Pete to let him audition that afternoon. She bounded in the room, hair ribbons flying, and announced,

"Pete! Telephone!"

"Cripes, Audrey, can't you see Jim here is trying to audition?" Pete growled as he left the room to take the call.

"Oh," she responded meekly, peering through her bangs at him, "I'm sorry."

His irritation was replaced with interest when he got a look at her up close. "It's fine," he smiled.

She smiled, and to him a ray of sun had burst brilliantly into the room. She turned and headed back up the stairs, and he noticed she blushed when she turned her head halfway up and smiled at him again.

Two weeks later he got his notice. He got in his '29 Ford and rushed right over to her house. He ran his hand through his hair nervously while he waited for someone to come to the door. He heard the lock turn, and she threw the door open and breathlessly said, "Jim! What a nice surprise!

Come in!" He looked into her eyes, and she softly said, "What's wrong?"

"Can we sit in the parlor?"

"Of course," she responded as she led him to the floral sofa.

They sat, and he took both her hands in his. "Audrey, these couple of weeks have been the best I have ever had." He looked into her eyes. "I...." He looked down. She let go of his hand, placed her fingers under his chin, and drew his eyes back to her own. "Tell me," she whispered. He gathered his courage and blurted, "I love you." She let out a deep breath and said, "What a relief. I thought it was something horrible." She smiled, squeezed his hands and said, "I love you, too." Her smile faded when she saw that it was not returned. "What?" she spoke, placing her forehead against his.

He knew then that he would never forget this moment. It was the most perfect and the absolute worst at the same time. He would remember her smell, the feel of her hair against his forehead, the way their knees touched, the color of the flowers on the sofa. He hesitated, clasped her hands harder and looking her gently in the eye said, "I've been drafted. I have to report for basic training in three days." She gasped, covered her mouth with her hand, and he saw the tears beginning to form in her eyes. She recovered quickly and said, "Fine. We have no choice, do we?" She smiled, even though the tears were still there, squared her shoulders and announced, "We will make three days seem like three years."

The bus rolled away from the curb, and he watched her wave until she was out of sight. It was the picture that he

81

carried into battle, through the agony that was World War II. Letters from her arrived sporadically, several days without them and then a flurry of two or three in a single day. She wrote every day, declaring her love, and he carried them with him all through war-torn France. He wrote as often as he could, and in one letter she informed him that her brother was also in France. It was still a surprise when Pete turned up, an addition to his unit. They became like brothers, spending countless hours in foxholes and in French watering holes when on leave. It was in a small café that Pete met Marie, a beautiful young woman. Pete fell fast and hard. Several months later, Pete pulled Jim aside.

"Jim, I've got to talk to you," he whispered as he led Jim to his tent.

They stepped inside, and Jim said, "Talk."

"On my next day's pass, Marie and I are going to get married."

Jim smiled and slapped Pete on the back. "That's great." He wanted to ask why so quickly, but with the ever-present danger of death, many men married as soon as they could.

Pete sat down. "I would have waited until the war was over, but we can't," he said as he looked Jim in the eye. "Marie is pregnant."

"I understand."

"I need to ask you...well, you are like a brother to me. If...if...anything happens to me, will you take care of Marie and the baby?"

Jim smiled. "Of course, Pete."

Pete returned the smile. "I knew that I could count on you."

Jim looked as bad as he felt. The time he had been dreading had come. He knocked on the door of Marie's home, hat in hand. The door flung open and Marie appeared.

"Hallo, Jeem." She looked over his shoulder and smiled back at him. "Where is my Peter hiding?"

"Can I come in, Marie?"

She paled visibly and let him in. He followed her to another room and sat down in the chair she offered him. "Marie," he began, but she began to cry.

"I already know what you have come to tell me, Jeem," she choked through her sobs. "My Peter, he has died, is that not true?"

Jim nodded. "If there is anything I can do, tell me, Marie."

She looked up. "You know of my problem, yes?"

He nodded again.

She leaned close and whispered. "Perhaps you do not know that I live here with my Aunt and Uncle, who will not be kind when they discover my problem. Can you help me get to the United States? I could raise my child there, in the land of his father."

"I promise that I will, Marie."

Jim found the only way to get a French citizen to America during the war was to marry her. He gave it much thought and decided that desperate times called for desperate measures. They were married in a quick ceremony, with the understanding that once Marie reached the United States and gave birth, she would apply for divorce, leaving Jim free to return and propose to Audrey.

He didn't feel it was right to explain all of this to

Audrey in a letter. Three months after he put his bride on a ship for the United States, he followed her across the Atlantic, home at last. He cabled that he was coming, both his parents and Marie, and found them all waiting when he burst through the door.

"God, it's good to be home," he sighed, as he was hugged by his mother. Marie gave him a hug, and his father shook his hand. When Marie left the room, his mother said, "You had another visitor."

"Who? No one knew I was coming."

"Audrey."

His heart plummeted to the bottom of his stomach. "Did she meet Marie?" he asked, attempting to be as casual as possible.

"Of course, I introduced her to your wife."

After Jim and Marie explained the entire situation to his parents, he rushed over to Audrey's house.

She opened the door, scowling.

"What do you want?"

"To explain."

"You don't need to. I've seen your wife. Congratulations on the expectant arrival." The door slammed in his face. He knocked again and kept knocking for ten minutes, but she would not answer the door.

"Don't worry, Jeem. I will talk to your Audrey and make everything right again," were Marie's words as she left the house. Jim paced nervously until his father said, "Sit, son. Nothing much you can do but wait."

The door opened and Marie came in, tears still clinging to the corner of her eyes. "I am sorry, Jeem. She would not listen. She would not believe that I loved her brother and that it is his child that I am carrying. But do not give up. She loves you very much still."

He clung to that hope until he heard that Audrey married Bill Phillips, a returning Air Force pilot. He had tried for six months, after his divorce and after the birth of the baby, which Marie had named Peter. It still wasn't enough to convince Audrey of his honorable deed.

And now she was gone. He had moved to Chicago after her wedding, and threw himself into a profitable career as a Marketing Director. He occasionally dated, but never let them get serious. He kept up with her life through his parents and his subscription to the Battle Creek Enquirer. It was there that he learned of the birth of her children, their school successes, their weddings, and the births of her grandchildren. Once, he made a trip to California to visit Marie and Peter. Peter was a handsome young man, the image of his father. Marie had married a fine man and was very happy. So, too, was Audrey, it seemed. He stayed out of her life until he boarded the plane to attend her funeral.

Three weeks after the funeral, he opened the door to his apartment to find Audrey's son standing there.

"Jim?"

"Yes, Wayne. Come in."

"So you know who I am, then."

"Of course."

Jim led him into the living room and showed him a seat.

"Can I get you anything to drink?"

"No. I'm here on behalf of my mother."

"I assumed as such."

Jim sat as Wayne continued. "I promised mother that I would come as soon as I could after her funeral. She was ill for quite a while. She told me about you, and my Uncle Pete, and Marie."

"I see," Jim replied.

"What you don't know is that Marie and her son Peter came to visit Mother about thirty years ago. She said that she took one look at that boy and knew that what you had tried to convince her of all those years ago was true. She said he was the image of his father. But by that time, it was too late."

"But after your dad passed. Why didn't she call then?"

"She was already sick by that time. I told her that I would find you and bring you to her, but she was emphatic that I not. She didn't want you to see her that way."

Jim looked Wayne right in the eye. "I wouldn't have cared. I loved her. Still do."

"I know. But she had her pride, and I wouldn't go against her wishes."

He reached in his pocket and presented Jim with an envelope. "This is from her. I want you to know, too, that I admire you for what you did. I loved my father, but he and my mother never shared something as deep as what the two of you had." He stood. "I'll be going. I think you need to read that alone."

Jim stood also and approached Wayne with outstretched arms. Clasping him in a hug, he choked, "You will never know what it means to me - you coming here and saying the things that you did. I never meant any disrespect to your father. From what I heard, he was a fine man."

Wayne returned the hug, pulled back and said, "You

gave him more respect than anyone in this world ever did by letting my mother live her life."

He walked to the door. "Take care. If you ever visit Battle Creek, look me up."

The door closed softly and Jim went back to his seat and looked at the envelope. His name was written on the front in her familiar hand. He tenderly ran his finger across it, then turned it over and opened it. He pulled out the paper, unfolded it and read.

March, 1996

Dear Jim:

If you are reading this then my time on this earth must be finished. I have asked my son, Wayne, to deliver this personally so you must have met him. I have told him of our situation and he understands perfectly.

I have met Marie's son, and he is the exact image of my brother Pete. I realized when I did that everything that you tried to tell me all those years ago was true. I was a foolish young woman with a broken heart, who felt that she had been horribly wronged. I thought that if I married someone else, I would forget about you. But I have not. If it is possible, I love you more now than I ever could. My late husband was a good and faithful man, but you have always held a prominent place in my heart. I never laid eyes on you again after my wedding, but your image is burned in my heart and in my soul. I am confident that someday we will be together again, probably in the next life. I guarantee that I will be waiting for you on the other side, my love, and nothing will ever separate us again.

I will love you for eternity,
Audrey

Tears dripped on the paper, but a smile was on his face. She loved him after all. It was enough.

'Ig 'Oy

Fred Thornburg

It wasn't the type of news that normally caught her eye. She usually skimmed through the paper, nothing more than an early morning formality. Check out the headlines, get enough of the details so she could cruise through the discussions at work. They thought she was on top of the local events, a regular Yankee Doodle civic-minded citizen, and she had been, at first. She had tried to keep up with it all. Local news, charities, volunteering, being the open door at work where you could always drop in and unload your problems. As head of personnel, or rather "Human Resources," for Twin City Health Care, it was her job. In fact, she would often make the papers herself at ribbon cutting ceremonies, wearing a company tee shirt covered with sweat from a 5 K run, or playing donkey basketball in the high school gym against the Mayor and his team. She had a hand in everything. But really, one can only do so much. From the breakfast meeting to the late night city council meetins, she was thinning out. She had always given it her all, but that just made them ask for more. Now it seemed she could give nothing her complete attention.

> Fred Thornburg is an electronics technician who works in a professional atmosphere. While he is repairing equipment, he is also listening. The results are stories based in the real world. Fred has always enjoyed writing as an outlet.

The only thing that had drawn her total attention for more than a minute in the last ten years was this little article on page three, section C. She had turned to the Local News page, scanning the obituaries, when she saw it: "Local Landmark Turned Eyesore To Be Torn Down." The paragraph went on to tell how the Big Boy on Third Street, first in the national chain, would soon be torn down to make way for an adult living center. She read the small article then sat staring at the paper. Those trickling into the early morning Kiwanis breakfast meeting thought she was intently studying the local current events. But the events she was concentrating on weren't local, or current.

What was it thirty, thirty-five years ago? Thirty-seven years ago. She was a twelve-year-old girl. Not old enough to get the whole picture, but old enough to tell that something was wrong. Being an only child meant you spent more time focusing on your parents. There were fewer diversions as there would be in a large family. Thinking back, she had not been surprised when she was sent to spend the summer with her Aunt Gertrude near the farm where her mother had been raised. As her career advanced and her Day Planner filled up, the memory of that summer had been pushed to the back like a letter labeled: "Not Urgent: Read At Your Convenience, If Ever." Although not convenient, here it was, spreading out in her mind.

Aunt Gert and Uncle Ed Klogziem. She had enjoyed the Sunday visits to their little farm, but living there was a different matter. Sally had never really had any responsibility, no chores were needed to get what she wanted. Just some well-timed tears, whining, or a screaming fit would do the trick. But not at Aunt Gert's. Here Sally was in charge of the chickens. Tears, tantrums, and whining had no effect on Aunt Gert. In fact, it had the opposite effect.

That summer had been a crash course in work ethics,

responsibilities, and chickens. She got her first blister that summer and had cried herself to sleep the first week. As if dealing with her parents' separation was not enough, now the smell of chicken shit hung in the hot, humid air. And like her terrible situation, it would not go away.

And now, looking back, Sally was starting to see that sometimes the more frustrating the situation is, the more rewarding the outcome. Aunt Gert and Uncle Ed had, without her knowing it, opened her eyes to a different way of life. She saw for the first time that she had control of her future. She saw that hard work yielded its own rewards. And it was the little story in the paper that brought her back to this lesson.

At first she cursed her chores: getting up at sunrise to lug feed out to the chickens, collecting eggs, cleaning the coop, hauling water while all the other kids were still in bed or getting up to eat cereal and watch TV. Then she would go in and have, what else, eggs and bacon for breakfast. Then it was out to the garden with Aunt Gert to weed and water, and listen to her rambling on the good old days. Then it was lunch of, what else, fresh fruit and veggies. To be followed by more work, more talk, and on and on, same routine, until Saturday. Saturday started just as early. But instead of harvesting the garden they harvested the chickens. The first such Saturday saw Sally staring innocently at the chopping block where Uncle Ed stood, hatchet poised, with a chicken lying silently under his grasp.

"What do you think we feed them for, charity? Haven't you ever thought about this as you sit down at your fancy table and have chicken for Sunday dinner? It's just a fact of life; if not for our need to eat it, this here chick woulda' never been born. And no, I do not specifically enjoy it; yes, it makes me a little sad. But it makes me enjoy the time they live with us that much more. I feel sorrier for you and Gert, 'cause you gotta' clean'em." And even now, twenty-seven years later, she could still remember that first bird. The hatchet's dull thud against the stump top, followed by a few moments of panicked shrieking, then silence. The feel of the already humid air getting moister from the boiling pot set out, and the smell of the wet feathers stuck on everything; she was sure she would never be clean of them

Sally sat, thinking back to those days, and to her present position as head of personnel. When it came to laying somebody off she had told her daughter, "No, I do not enjoy doing it; yes, it makes me a little sad. But if we had not hired them in the first place, they would not have worked at all." It had been so long since the first time she had said this that, until now, she'd forgotten where she had first heard it. They were similar chores, and although hers didn't smell as bad, the thought lingered on for an uncomfortably long time.

Sally sat through the Kiwanis meeting; her mind miles and years away. She had been so busy driving her career forward that she not taken the time to pause and look back. At the end of the meeting she left, wondering how many others had been there in body only. She called her office and canceled her afternoon meetings and drove out to the Golden Years Aged Care Facility. She had put off visiting Aunt Gert for the last seven years. Suddenly, she could see nowhere more important to be.

"Aunt Gert, it's me. Aunt Gert, it's Sally." If not for the name on the door, Sally would've still been looking for Aunt Gert. It seemed to her, that as a child changes drastically in seven years, so had Aunt Gert. This, plus the fact that on the one-hour drive over, she had been recalling the Aunt Gert from years past had led to the surprise at Gert's aged appearance. The lady that had been forever deeply tanned, able to hoist a five-gallon bucket of water over the rail fence now looked like she would have trouble lifting up her Styrofoam cup of water. She looked out of place lying in a bed. Gone was her blue dress, her denim apron, her sweat- stained straw hat. Gone were those old leather boots and brown jersey work gloves. Gone was the old hoe she always carried, as much a walking cane as a garden tool. Gone was any character. Here, in this generic metal bed, in yet another white room, dressed in the mass-laundered green smock, she looked like just another set of eyes, glazed over and looking at nothing, just viewing the past. "Aunt Gert, it's Sally." Gertrude's face twisted for a moment, as though she couldn't tell why the voice in her thoughts sounded so clear.

"Don't play tricks on an old lady. Who's there, I ask ya. Damn kids. Don't trick me, I warn ya."

"Aunt Gert, it is me, Sally. You musta' been sleeping with your eyes open. I thought I'd stop by and see how you were doing."

"Sally? Sally Karcher? Lord, is that really you? Come over closer here, it is you! My Lord girl, look at you. Are you all right? You look awfully thin. And what you all dressed up for, to see me? I hope you ain't sick, or all dressed up to bring me bad news. You can't be here to tell me someone's died, cause everybody I know's dead already. All 'cept me. And if you come to tell me I'm dead, I knowed I be in heaven if I'm gettin' to see you again. Did you stop by to hear an old lady ramble on? I didn't think so. Now what's on your mind, Little Sally?"

"I don't know, Aunt Gert. I was just thinkin', I mean thinking about the past, about staying with you and Uncle Ed, and I just thought I'd come by. I haven't thought about that summer for awhile, and I guess I feel a little ashamed at not stopping by to see you. I just now realized that I haven't seen you since Ed's funeral. Sorry it took so long."

"Sally, maybe I can tell you why it took so long for you to come. I'm betting you're just now gittin' to know yourself. What's that look for? You know what I mean. We all go through it. Some people know themselves at age five, some at twenty-five, some at seventy-five. Some, maybe never. Me, I wandered around in circles for a few years, chasing dreams others had made up for me. When I looked for direction, all I could see was what others wanted me to see, or rather sell me. Everything I read, listened to, people I talked to had their own agenda. Seems like roping me in was their goal. Then, almost overnight, I realized the only person with my best interest in mind was, surprise, me. Now this don't mean I'm selfish, no way. Part of being me is helping others, just the way I helped your mother when she broke up with your daddy. Neither one of them was at fault, neither one was a bad person. They just didn't know themselves. And how can you hope to know others if you don't know yourself? That summer we kept you, that was a good summer."

"I can still see your face, oh, your eyes, when Ed killed that first bird. You stood like an oak till that hatchet came down, then it was like lightning hit you. You went damn near as wild as that bird. Ed stood there with a dead bird in one hand, that hatchet in the other, and an embarrassed look on his face. You worked hard that summer, Sally. Not at first, but by the end of the summer, you was workin' like a twenty year old. Cleaning them birds, setting in the hot sun at the market all day Saturday. Then on the way home we'd stop at the Big Boy and get you a big sundae. Remember the first time we went there? I remember Ed sayin', 'Sally, you worked hard this

94

week. How 'bout Gert and me takin' you over to the 'ig 'oy.'
Just like that he said it, thinkin' that was really the name of the
place. You burst out laughin', thought you was fit to pee right
there in the parking lot. That was the first laugh, the first smile
we'd seen all week. Old Ed had that same embarrassed look on
his face, till you told him about the light bulbs being burned out
on part of the sign. Then Ed laughed harder 'en I'd seen him
laugh in awhile. Wound up going there every Saturday night,
didn't we? Yeah, that was a good summer. Took you from a
spoiled brat to a hard worker we was proud of. Another few
months and we would'a had you knowing yourself. But, I guess
we planted the seed. And I guess now, that seed has grown and
blossomed. Sally, I think back to that summer often. But what
else do I have to do?"

"I miss our little house, guess it's for sale again. I miss
my garden, I miss the beautiful fall sunrises, and the still
summer sunsets. I miss the sound of the birds out in the wheat
field, the sound of the rain on the tin roof of the chicken coop.
I miss the taste of the sweet corn right out of the field, eating
blueberries as we picked them. You know, I even miss the
smell of the chicken shit, the sound of that back door screen
slamming as you'd go out for your morning chores, and the
smell of diesel smoke from Ed's tractor. And Ed, I miss him so.
In here, it's the same green light, the same bleached out smell,
the same bland lunch everyday. I hear the same people
muttering incoherently, or screaming to get them out. It's
always the same. All the money we'd saved, all the possessions
we'd collected, all that I was proud of, is gone. And here I sit
in this white, cinderblock room. But Sally, there's one thing I
have, that's my memories. I am comfortable with myself, and
I got my memories. Guess I shouldn't complain. Like Ed used
to say, 'Life's like a diaper, you can either put up with the shit

or change it, but crying won't make it any better.' Anyway, Sally, I'm kinda' tired now, I wanna' get back to my memories."

Her drive back to town gave her time to think, time she normally didn't have. What memories would she have in the white room when she reached that point? Of nights and weekends spent in meetings? Of arguments with her husband as they raced to climb the corporate ladders? Of the time she spent trying to get her own two kids to do something constructive, something at all? She was collecting the possessions, but why? Because that's what the media said people like her did. People who didn't know themselves, who were sold the dreams of others. She'd been putting on a show for years, doing it all for other people. Putting up with shit. Maybe it was time she changed the diaper.

On her drive back she made two calls: one to her secretary to place an ad in the paper for a Head of Human Relations. The other to a friend, or now that she looked closer, a contact, in the real estate market. "Dan, this is Sally. Say, I'd like to talk to you about buying the old Klogziem farm. Yes, this afternoon. And Dan, I know you've got friends downtown. Can you get me a corner booth out of the Big Boy before they tear it down? Thanks. Oh, some day you'll understand."

A Golden Summer

Millie Ball

It was summer in Cape Harbor, Maine, a small town, and my favorite time of year. I had a summer job in a real estate office and was going to our community college. Life was wonderful but quiet until summer came each year and then it seemed to be overrun with people, all coming down from the cities to vacation in our quaint little town.

Liz was working at the real estate office on Saturday morning when this impressive white haired man appeared in front of her desk. "Good morning, sir, may I help you?" "Yes indeed, I am looking for a rental by the sea for the summer. Do you have any listings I can look at?"

Liz looked him over carefully: *my, his clothes look worn and he is so thin, I wonder where he came from? He looks just like Mark Twain, white beard and all.* "Well, yes, we have a lot of rentals, but no one is here to help right now; they are all out showing homes to rent. Can you come back on Monday?"

"No, no, I need something right now. I just got off the bus and want a place today, not on Monday."

Millie Ball was born in Detroit, Michigan, but has lived in Petoskey, Michigan for over 40 years. She is married, has one son and one grandson. She has worked for over 40 years as an office manager, secretary, bookkeeper, and retired from a C.P.A. office as an executive secretary.

97

Liz thought for a minute: *I wonder if he couldn't rent Aunt Ethel's cottage? It's right on the sea shore and she is away for the summer. She probably could use the money, should I? Yes, I think I will.* "Well, you are in luck. It just so happens my Aunt has a cottage that would suit you just fine, and it is available right now. By the way, what is your name sir?"

"I am T. J. Treadwell, and young lady you have a quick mind to come up with a solution to my problem so fast."

"Oh, good, I am Liz Foster. My mother and I live here in Cape Harbor, and I am very happy to meet you and if you can wait 30 minutes I will close the office; we close at noon on Saturdays; we can go over and look at it then."

"That's agreeable young lady. Can I just sit here by the window and wait?"

"Oh yes, that's fine. I'll clear my desk and finish what I need to do." She quickly went into the back office and called her mother to verify what she had done was going to be all right with Aunt Ethel.

"Liz, that's a wonderful idea! You know Aunt Ethel needs the money and it never occurred to either of us to rent the cottage."

"There, Mr. Treadwell, I'm finished. My car is just outside. Let's get your bags and we'll be on our way." They drove along the shore to the cottage. The winding road was filled with wild flowers and cedar trees, it was breath-taking. Mr. Treadwell thought so too, Liz could tell. He never took his eyes off the view of the sea or the landscape. They arrived at the cottage and it too was beautiful; Aunt Ethel has always kept the yard filled with flowers and bushes. As they entered the cottage, Liz had almost forgotten how light and fresh the cottage was, there was light streaming in the windows making uneven designs all over the walls in beautiful colors and the smell of flowers from the yard filled the room. It was enchanted, she thought.

"Well my dear, this is indeed a delightful place. Let's look upstairs." The two bedrooms upstairs were just as homey and decorated as if someone lived in every room at this very minute. "Yes," said Mr. Treadwell, "this will do, now let's talk about the rent."

The rent, yes, the rent. Let's see the rent. I know he can't afford much. He needs new clothes and probably doesn't have money to buy food.

"How about $200.00 a month and that will include all utilities."

"$200.00 a month? Are you sure?"

"Yes, yes, quite sure. It needs cleaning and it is some distance from the main road, so $200.00 a month is fair."

"All right, young lady, I'll pay the full three months right now and since I have my bags with me, I will move in now."

"Fine, I'll take you to the market and you can get some food supplies and I will come by now and then to keep you company and see if you need anything." They put his bags upstairs and went to the market where Liz picked out every thing she thought he would need to put some weight on. But when they came to pay for all of the groceries she wondered if he had enough money. He did which surprised Liz but then many things in her life were that way. After she helped him put the groceries away, she left for home to tell her mother all about her latest adventure: she knew for sure this would be another Golden Summer. Most of her summers were this way, as she had a way of making them so.

The next morning was Sunday and after church Liz drove over to check on Mr. Treadwell. He was sitting on the porch reading. "Hi, Mr. T., beautiful day, isn't it?" "Yes, surely it is, Liz."

"I want to show you something, Mr. T." She disappeared into the kitchen and soon came back with a basket full of food. "Come on, I have a secret place, and I want you to see it." They walked along the beach for awhile and soon some sand dunes appeared. "There, over there," she called. There was a small cave right in the dunes and almost hidden from view. "I come here a lot, Mr. T. It is so quiet and I can sit and watch the waves and just dream." Mr. T. laughed and agreed with Liz that it was special indeed. They sat and watched the sea roll its waves upon the sand, crashing at times over the large rocks. As the sun was almost ready to set, they went down to the beach and Liz gathered wood for a large fire. After it was blazing and red hot they carved roasting sticks out of twigs she found and roasted hot dogs, ate fruit, drank ice tea and watched the stars as they appeared almost all at once.

"Liz, I have not enjoyed myself this much in many a year, thank you so much."

"Oh, Mr. T. this is the way life is here in Cape Harbor. We live a quiet peaceful life and love it."

"I envy you, Liz. If only I could spend my remaining years here."

"You can, you can. I can arrange for a rental for you anytime and perhaps even Aunt Ethel's cottage for a few more months."

"That's kind of you, Liz, but it is quite impossible. I have many things to take care of in New York."

"Oh, you're from New York; I wondered where you came from. Do you like New York?"

"It's all I know, it's my way of life."

Poor man, thought Liz, *I bet he lives in an old folks' home or something like that. I will make this summer one he will never forget.* And that she did, there were many hot dog roasts on the beach, clam bakes, walks in the woods, quiet times at the cottage reading to him. Why one time she almost got him on a bicycle.

As summer was drawing to a close and Liz knew he had to leave in a few days, she planned a big going-away party for him. Mom agreed to help; she also had grown very fond of Mr. T.

"Now let's see. We'll ask Carl from the Market, Mr. T. has formed a real relationship with him. They talk for hours every time he shops. And Clara, she not only cleans for him but she too enjoys just being around him. He has a way of making you feel wanted and useful. We'll get clams and lobster; you can make potato salad and I'll make a glorious cake. He loves my cakes you know." So the day before his departure, she broke the news that a big party was in the making, and Mr. T. was happy and delighted to be a guest at such a fine affair. He laughed quietly to himself, he knew Liz loved planning these cookouts. Well, they did have a wonderful party and the weather cooperated completely; it couldn't have been more perfect. After they gathered up the leftovers, they all said good bye to Mr. T. Liz said she would be by in the morning to drive him to the bus station.

Liz arrived early and helped Mr. T. get his bags packed. They both were very quiet. It was evident they had become very close friends and each knew saying goodbye was not going to be easy. As they drove to the bus station Liz asked if she could reserve the cottage for next summer. "No, my dear, I am afraid not. It was hard to get away this summer and next summer would probably be more difficult." The bus was right on time and she gave him a big hug but could not speak; her eyes were flooded with tears that choked her words. But Mr. T. knew what she wanted to say.

"I can never thank you enough, Liz, for the most wonderful summer of my life; I shall never forget it or you. Take care of yourself and finish college, its important to you and to me." With that he boarded the bus and Liz stood for a long time watching it disappear down the long winding road. She slowly went back home knowing in her heart things would never quite be the same again.

Fall came and college began - her final year. She majored in education, always wanting to be a teacher but would no doubt have to accept a position elsewhere in the state as Cape Harbor only had two small schools.

Winter and spring came and summer was almost here. She wondered if Mr. T. would be back. He never came and she never saw him again.

"Get Jason in here," yelled Mr. Treadwell.

"Now, now, steady Mr. Treadwell. I am the nurse in charge here, and I'll not allow you to get yourself all worked up and shouting orders."

"Listen here young lady," barked Mr. Treadwell, "I want to see Jason and you get him here right now or you'll be looking for another job."

"Well, if that's what you want," stormed his nurse, "I'll phone him at once but for goodness sake get control of yourself; you're going to have another heart attack."

Mr. Treadwell was owner of Treadwell Publishing, a very well-known and profitable publishing company in New York, a multi-million dollar business. Jason, a young man who Mr. Treadwell had hired ten years before and had taught him the publishing business after he graduated from college, was the President of the company. He was clever, ambitious, and most of all dedicated to Mr. Treadwell; he loved the kindly old man with all of his heart. He was more of a son to him than an employee. He had known for some time that Mr. Treadwell was ill and would not be with them much longer.

As he entered the bedroom of Mr. Treadwell's home, which was more of an estate, he could see that he was failing much quicker than he had anticipated. He had tried not to think about his dying, but today he couldn't put those thoughts off any longer; he could see the end would soon come.

"Good morning, sir. I got here as soon as I could, traffic was heavy as usual."

"Yes, I know, Jason. I want to go over some things with you and Kirk. Some time ago I changed my will and I want you to know about it before it is read to you after my funeral. As you know, Jason, I am leaving the company to you, seeing I have no children and my dear wife is now gone, but I am leaving only 51 percent of it to you and 49 percent to someone very dear to me, someone I met one summer when I was gone on vacation for three months. Now I know this will be hard for you to understand, you are going to think she is a stranger and knows nothing about the publishing business, but give her a chance, she is just what the company needs and I owe her more than I could ever repay. She gave me back three months of my lost youth. Nothing you can say will change my mind so try to make the best of it. There is enough for both of you, and who knows, it may even work out."

Jason could hardly believe what he was hearing. *Who in the world is this creature? She must have wound him around her finger or brainwashed him.* He was really upset but tried not to show it.

"Of course Tom, if this is what you want, then that's the way it is going to be."

"I appreciate that Jason. You and Kirk can work out the details; he has the changes in the will and I want Liz to be notified after my death not before."

Jason spent the next day checking out Liz Foster. His only disappointment was he could not find anything detrimental in her character. He even had Kirk Alexander, Mr. Treadwell's attorney, investigating her and he also came up blank.

Early on Monday morning Mr. Treadwell passed away quietly in his sleep. His nurse found him and called Jason and Kirk. The funeral was small and only close friends came, just as he wanted. Jason took the next couple of days off to try to get himself back together. He and Tom Treadwell had been very close and he would miss him more than he ever dreamed. He waited until the next morning to have Kirk notify Liz Foster of her inheritance.

Liz was in the living room trying to put together a résumé for a teaching job at one of the city's large schools when the door bell rang. *Why does that bell ring every time I am busy with something important?* She opened the door and there stood Mr. Alexander, tall, impressive, briefcase in hand.

Another insurance salesman, Liz thought.

"Yes, may I help you?"

"I am looking for Liz Foster."

"Yes, I am Liz Foster."

"I am Mr. Alexander, Mr. Thomas Treadwell's attorney. I have some things to discuss with you. May I come in?"

"Mr. Treadwell's attorney? You must be joking, he could never afford an attorney. Are you sure you have the right Liz Foster and the right Thomas Treadwell? The Mr. Treadwell that rented our cottage a couple or summers ago?"

"Yes, I know this is a shock to you but you are the right Liz Foster and I am indeed speaking of the Mr. Treadwell that rented from you." Liz just stood there, perhaps in shock, maybe a little inquisitive, but just stood there.

"May I come in?" asked Mr. Alexander?

"Oh, yes, please do. Forgive me, but this is hard to believe. He was so poor, and I just can't believe he had the money to have an attorney. What has happened to him, is he ill?"

"Well, to begin with, Mr. Treadwell was not a poor man. He was the founder and owner of Treadwell Publishing Company of New York, a multi-million dollar business. He has passed away, and you are named in his will as co-owner of his business."

"Me, me, inheriting part of his business? Why, I hardly knew him; we spent a good deal of time together that summer, and I really did love this dear gentlemen, but that's all."

"Yes I know, he told me all about you many times and the wonderful summer he had here. He never forgot it or you and found in you something he wished he had had in his youth: he found honesty, love, concern, beauty, all of that in you and wanted you to have more out of life than what you had here, financially I mean. The reading of the will is tomorrow and I will purchase a ticket for a flight out of here in the morning for you and would like you to be in New York by 1:00 p.m. tomorrow. Would that work out for you, Ms. Foster?"

"Well, I guess so," Liz replied slowly. This still had not completely sunk in.

"All right then, I will see you in New York. There will be a driver at the airport to pick you up." He then left and Liz was still trying to sort all of this out when her mother returned from shopping.

"Mom, you are not going to believe in a million years what has happened to me." She went into detail all about the conversation with Mr. Alexander and about the trip to New York. Her mother was a little apprehensive about the whole thing but thought Liz should go and see what it was all about. She packed her bags early in the morning and after breakfast her mother drove her to the airport.

She arrived in New York at noon, and sure enough there was a page for her as she departed the terminal. A driver was indeed there to take her to Treadwell Publishing Building. As they drove along the streets of New York, Liz could see that this was an entirely different world than she was used too and really didn't know if she liked it or not. Maybe she would refuse the offer and not take any inheritance and just go back to Cape Harbor. *We will see,* she told herself, and she continued to look at all the great buildings and high towers and busy streets filled with cars and people. *Where in the world are they all going and where did they come from?*

After a short drive they arrived at Treadwell Building and Carol, Mr. Treadwell's personal secretary, was there to meet her.

"Hi, Liz, I am Carol and I am here to help you in any way I can. Come, let's park your bags, and I'll have someone bring them up later. We'll go up and look around a bit before the meeting. Have you had lunch?"

"Yes, on the plane, thank you," Liz replied. *Carol seemed sure of herself* thought Liz *and very polite.*

"Come here Liz, this is or was Mr. Treadwell's office." It was large and just like a big business man's office should look: leather chairs and sofa, large tables, and a magnificent view that was overlooking Wall Street. *What a sight* she thought.

"My, Carol, I am impressed," said Liz. "This is totally different than I thought any office would be." She sat down for only a few minutes when Kirk came in and said the meeting was to begin. They all went into the conference room and there, already seated, was Jason. She looked directly at him and smiled, wondered who he was, and admitted to herself he was quite handsome.

"Good afternoon Liz. I am Jason, President of the Company, and I understand that we will share ownership of the business." His voice was cold and direct.

Oh boy, am I in for a battle. He doesn't like me and doesn't even know me. I bet he intended to have the entire company not half of it. Mr. Alexander read the Will and as he told her in Cape Harbor, Jason had inherited 51 percent of the company and she 49 percent. Jason inherited the home and all of his other assets which amounted to a sizeable amount. *There must be a good reason he left me so much of the company so I am going to apply myself and see what makes this place tick.* After the reading of the will, Carol took Liz to an apartment she had rented for her, if indeed she chose to remain in New York. Or would she sell her share of the company to Jason?

After getting Liz settled in her apartment, Carol suggested they shop and get Liz new clothes and a new hair style. Liz thought what she had was sufficient and the way she looked was fine, but Carol convinced her that New York and Cape Harbor were not exactly the same. New Yorkers were a different type of people to be sure. Liz agreed and went to have her "make-over," as Carol put it, and Liz did confess she now looked in part like a New Yorker. They shopped all day and found some very stylish clothes and Liz fell into the buying trap quite easily. She was shocked at the price of her wardrobe, but Carol had convinced her she could well afford it.

Monday morning came and Liz arrived at the office on time looking very sheik. Carol hardly recognized her as she approached her desk.

"Hi Carol, pretty cool huh?" Carol laughed and said Jason would be shocked - to say the least - and that he was waiting for her in his office. Liz knocked on Jason's door and went in. He was sitting at his desk and never looked up, just said, "I will be with you in a minute." Liz sat down and waited. She glanced around the room and could get a brief picture of what he was like. He had sail boats all over the walls; one handsomely carved on his bookshelves. She could tell he loved sailing. The room was very masculine. "Well,

Liz," Jason looked up and could not take his eyes off of her for a few moments. She was lovely he thought. Whatever she did to herself was a great improvement. "Well, Liz, as you know nothing about the publishing world and probably hate New York, I have decided to buy you out at a very good profit. I'll have Kirk draw up the papers and by tomorrow you can be on your way home."

"Now just a minute here," said Liz. "Who said anything about my wanting to sell my shares. Mr. Treadwell seemed to think I would be good for the company, maybe bring new life into it. Of course, I know nothing about the publishing business, but I can learn and if you would get yourself off your high horse, you could teach me."

"My dear girl, I have better things to do than nurse-maid a country girl into the business world. Just take the money and run." At that remark Liz got up from her chair, slammed the door and went to her office.

"Huh, thinks I'm a dummy, sure he does. I wouldn't leave now if my life depended on it. He just made the biggest mistake of his life."

Liz and Carol decided to work and work hard at her learning the publishing business in "ten easy lessons." Over the next few weeks, Liz read books, manuscripts, poems, what ever Carol gave her to edit until her eyes felt they would drop out. At last she felt she was ready to review whatever Jason gave her. Of course it was a book, a big book, a very big book. She read it and read it again, tried to keep an open mind, made notes and finally felt she was ready to report to Jason.

Early the next morning she took her copy of the edited manuscript to Jason and sat down and waited for his comments. He carefully read over her remarks and, after what seemed hours, looked up and said, "It's exactly what I expected. This manuscript came from one of our finest authors. His works are always best sellers. Your comments indicate his work needs many changes and you indicate you would not publish this book. Let's face it Liz, you have no talent for this job. Once again I will buy your interest and you can return home." Liz could not believe her ears! How could she have been so wrong. In tears she picked up the manuscript and ran out of the office. Carol saw her and guided her into her office and sat her down.

"Liz, for heaven's sake, get control of yourself. So you made a mistake. This is going to happen over and over. It takes a long time to learn to edit and be good at it. Of course, if you are a wimp, go ahead and give up, but I think you can conquer this if you have patience."

"You're right; I am acting like a child," sobbed Liz. "Of course I can do this."

Liz and Carol spent many weeks going over manuscripts and editing until they finally thought Liz was ready to make decisions on her own. She picked a book and after several days was ready for the last time, she told herself, to give it to Jason and see what he thought about her comments.

This time was different, thank goodness. As he finished reading her comments, he looked up and smiled; Jason did not smile often. He said she had done a fine job, had come a long way and would indeed be a good editor one day.

Early one Saturday morning, Jason called and asked if she would like to go sailing along the sea shore and perhaps have dinner on the boat. *I wonder what he is up to* she asked herself but agreed to go. He picked her up and they went directly to the boat. It was a large beautiful sailing vessel. She had never been on such a boat. They sailed along the coast and she was beginning to get the feel of the sails and loved it. They docked just about sunset and went below to prepare dinner. Jason was indeed a good cook she discovered, one more of his amazing talents. As they were eating and watching the sun set she began to look his face over closely. *My, he is handsome and very kind and gentle when he wants to be.* Jason was thinking the same thing about Liz. After they docked the boat, he took her back to her apartment. At the door he took her face in his hands and kissed her. She should have been surprised but was thrilled instead, she was now dreaming of how this would end, she could even see her wedding plans in her mind and her heart was full of joy. Silently she was humming her favorite song. What a day. What a wonderful day. Another Golden Summer.

Voices of Michigan

The Answer Is in the Skyline

Angela Wennerberg-DuFay

I was near the county line when a strange thing happened. I caught a glimpse of a sparkling blue flash; the icy-cool blue of Lake Superior tempered with a brilliance of a far-away star — the color of my father's eyes.

It happened as I drove home after the funeral. I had just buried my father. He passed away suddenly; I didn't have a chance to say good-bye. As the miles passed, I was reminded of all of the things that I meant to say to him. *If I could just have ten more minutes. I swear I would tell him.*

I'm tired. I really need to stop the car and get out. Too much driving — not enough sleeping. I had spent the past 72 hours looking for answers. I pulled over to the shoulder and got out of the car. I took a long deep breath to try to clear my head. The smell of burnt rubber from rotting tires invaded my lungs as I tried not to breathe in the stench. I glanced up the road and saw a wrought-iron fence encasing

Angela Wennerberg-DuFay received both her B.S. and M.A. from Northern Michigan University in the field of English. She lives in Marquette with her husband and son. She has been published in *Above the Bridge* magazine.

113

what seemed to be a graveyard for cars. *How could I have missed that?* I had been so distracted that I had somehow missed seeing the pile of cars that I had passed.

I decided that I needed a walk. I grabbed my jacket and started up the road. The cars were about a half-mile up from where I had stopped. As I neared the puzzle of metal, I saw years of neglect. *I'm sorry Dad. I thought you'd always be here.* Amidst the maze of weeds were crumpled fenders, shattered headlights and sunken roofs. In and out of the labyrinth I trudged, as if in search of something. I wove my way past the cancer-eaten relics that had at one time been full of life. There seemed to be a pattern; almost a town set up for these cars to live out their remaining years. I turned to the right, and there were the seventies: Pintos and Mustangs, followed by the long, boat-like Cutlass Cieras. Around the corner were the beginnings of the eighties, with only a heap of Yugo's to prove the passage of time. As I walked past the mounds, confirming the years that had passed, I looked over to see the years of my father. A Thunderbird here, a Willey's Wagon there.

I needed to go. I had stayed longer than I thought. The outline of my car, parked down the road, could barely be seen. Vehicles raced by as I turned my sights on the highway and began to walk. It happened again. I saw my Dad's eyes sparkle. I stepped back, trying to fathom what was happening to me. I closed my eyes, took a deep breath and tried to regain my composure. I slowly opened my eyes and looked. Amidst the mangled, rusty bodies of Detroit's earlier years, I saw her: a 1956 Ford Crown Victoria Skyliner — my father's first car.

114

Dad had told me about how he first learned to fix cars. His neighbor, Mr. Cooney, had a garage next door to his house and with no sons of his own, Dad became his apprentice. He started out slow, learning how to fix tires and change oil. Slowly he worked up to fixing head gaskets and fine tuning brakes. Dad wanted me to learn the trade, too.

"Isn't that what garages are for, Dad? I can just drop it off and someone else does the dirty work. I don't have time for all that grease. Anyway, everything's computerized. None of that old stuff you used to do even works."

Unlike the rest of the cars, "Vicky" was seemingly showcased. All of the mangled bodies overlapped and encircled her, leaving her unscathed, with only sunlight penetrating her inner sanctum. I peered through a gap between the Buicks and the Cadillacs to get a closer look and wedged my body through the rusting fingers of sun-sharpened metal. Walking around her, I surveyed the damage: flat tires, dented rear panel, missing emblems, hanging door handles, antennae broken in half. Not bad. The glass top was still intact, as was the entire frame. The paint was a dust-rag gray. *I thought I had seen blue?!* As I walked past the front bumper on the driver's side, I accidentally hit it, knocking it loose from its unsteady grip. I bent down to try to replace it. There was the blue. The sun had faded the entire car. Had faded everything except for the places that had been hidden by the sun. *How did I see this from the road?*

Every Sunday morning during the summer, before it was un-cool to, Dad would get me out of bed to take me down to the lake to fish. I remember sitting on the pier with him. He dangled his feet in the water, while mine were safely

tucked beneath me. I told him that I was more comfortable
that way. Truth was, I didn't want the fish mistaking my toes
for bait. He always winked at me each time he asked. We
spent hours fishing and talking. His favorite stories were
about Vicky.

He was going to be a pianist, an artist, a poet. His
long, sleek fingers were deft enough to reach the most
demanding chords, yet slight enough to pencil in the shadows
of remorse into a fading sunset. His words were like roses,
blowing amongst the storms of life. But then everything
changed. He was drafted. His fingers no longer touched keys,
they tightened bolts, wrote communications and detailed
maps. He didn't mind, though. He was fixing cars again, and
learning more than Mr. Cooney could have ever taught him.
He told me that a mechanic was truly an artist that modeled
cars into fine pieces of machinery.

When my dad turned 15, Mr. Cooney called him over
to show him his latest project: a 1956 Vicky. She was only
seven years old, but looked more like a hundred. The owner
had never heard of oil and never thought of using a hose to
clean her. Mr. Cooney looked at my Dad and told him that
if he fixed her, he could have her. My father's hopes and
dreams began with that car. He had so many dreams and so
much that he was going to do.

*There was so much that I hadn't done. So many questions
unanswered. I had done so little for him during his lifetime.* It was
then that I decided to do something about it. Come
tomorrow morning, Vicky was going to come home.

The next morning was a lesson in futility. I called
every mechanic in the tri-county area trying to discover who

owned the junkyard that I had passed. One by one, I was
passed onto someone who thought they could help -- but
couldn't. After 20-or so helpers, I talked with a woman who
said her husband had owned the place, but he had just passed
away, so sorry, you'll have to wait out probate. . . I told her
that I understood and explained a bit of my story, thanked her
for her time and hung up. No sooner had I hung up when the
phone rang. She said her son would meet me at the yard with
the tow truck.

"What about the courts?" I asked.

"Screw'em," she said. "Some things are just more
important."

I'm just learning that for myself.

At 7:15, amidst the pouring rain and thunder, I pulled
up to the curb in front of my house and quickly jumped out.
I eagerly waved the tow truck into the drive. As gently as it
could, the rusted red truck lumbered up the slight incline of
the paved driveway. The garage door slowly opened to reveal
a few of my buddies that I had called from my car phone.
Their eyes lit up as the darkness invaded the well-lit room.
Step by slow, backward step, the car was put into place.

"You don't know the first thing about cars!" one said.
"Too bad your Dad's not around. Hell, he was good with his
hands."

I had tried working with Dad once. I was home from
school. My car wasn't running well. I had flipped open the
yellow pages and was thumbing through the Auto Body
section when my Dad came in.

"What are you doing with that? You don't have
money to pay some garage. All 'ya need is a tune-up," he said

as he grabbed the phone book and threw into the opened drawer. "C'mon."

"Dad, I don't know the first thing about -"

He cut me off, "I tried to show you."

"Dad, don't start with me." The fight ended in the garage.

"Here, take that wrench and loosen up that bolt."

"What bolt?"

He closed his eyes and took a deep breath and began again. This time his voice was gentler. He began to explain the inner-workings of an engine and then suddenly stopped. He must have been able to read my mind. He looked at me and said, "Here, you've got more important things to do. Take my keys and go visit your friends. I'll take care of this."

After the tow-truck left and everyone filtered out, I closed the garage door and gently opened Vicky's creaky door. I held it steady as I eased the hinges back into place. I firmly gripped the steering wheel. *Hello Dad. I want to get to know you.*

It was time.

I bought every manual that I could find, from Classic Motorbooks to basic engine repair. My bible became Cars & Parts magazine. It took weeks for me to compile her autopsy: pieces that needed to be replaced, fixed, overhauled or ordered. Each weekday was filled with calls to parts stores across the country, while my weekends were spent on dashes here and there to collect the parts. The mail carrier, who used to walk by my house, now began at my house -- he had to carry a few too many engine parts on his route for me.

As the pieces arrived, I would clean them up. I

removed old residues with a soft cloth, a chamois, and sometimes an old cloth diaper. Steel wool fit the bill on most rust, while the grinder was reserved for the most menacing corrosions.

"Why do you need to go away to the university? There's a good college here in town. You could stay here with mom and me and save a lot of money." The fight was one that we'd had most of my senior year. Though this would be the last time the subject would come up.

"Fine, Dad. I'll stay here and become nothing more than a bloody mechanic," I yelled defiantly.

He said nothing more. His crystalline blue eyes refused to look at me. He grabbed his red oil rag, wiped the dirt from the socket in his hand, and walked out of the garage.

Ashes to ashes, dust to dust -- I had lost so much. I'm getting rid of the past - paint, rust. . . bad memories.

I spent every spare minute assembling the bits and pieces I needed to resurrect Vicky. *Why didn't I spend this much time with you, Dad?* Each piece was laid to rest on old towels that were spread across the floor in the garage: coil springs, hydraulic shocks, aluminum pistons, wire wheel covers, door handle shields, rocker molding trim, and more. Everything that made a Crown Victoria Skyliner a "Vicky," took occupancy on the floor. As the garage became more cluttered in shiny silver metal, I learned to close my eyes when the flourescent lights came on. The glare from the polished parts was blinding.

Nearly two years passed since I first saw her. I finally had all of the pieces to my gigantic puzzle and began to put her together. My endless nights of Self-Taught Mechanics

101 were being put to the test. When pieces wouldn't fit, or when my knuckles bled too much from ripping them up against the innards of the engine, I'd work on the prep for the exterior, or look inside to mutter about the abuse the ole' girl had endured. I became obsessed. I went to work early, didn't eat lunch and raced home just to be with her.

Dad told me that Vicky broke down during a rainstorm one July. He had spent the rest of the summer lying underneath her trying to decode the memory of Mr. Cooney's instructions, and some days just napping.

He learned more in those two years in the Army motor pool then he had in the ten years working alongside Mr. Cooney. He anxiously called home one day to report that he knew how to bring Vicky back to life. But he was never able to get her running. Grandma had her towed away a month before the call. My father never had a chance to collect his dreams from inside that car. Hopes and ideas were locked inside of it forever.

Once pieced together, I decided that I had to let a body shop do the paint job. I didn't want the chassis looking like a new weekend mechanic had her. She was a beauty and deserved a full make over. At the garage, I described the color I wanted.

"You know the color of the sky where it meets the lake?" I asked. They thought that I was nuts.

"Sure buddy. But why don't you do us a favor. Go out to the lake and get us a sample of it, okay?" He laughed. "Look, we don't start paintin' 'til mornin'. Bring us back a real sample. Y'know? Like a swatch or somethin'."

Undaunted, I went to the paint store and looked

through palette upon palette, while a sympathetic clerk did her best to mix the right color. Nothing came close.

I went home and slumped at my desk. *Fine. Paint it any color. It doesn't matter.* I decided to leave a note for the mechanic on my way to work: "Paint it any color you want!" I searched my desk for a pen. No pens?! Leafing through the mass of papers on my desk, I shuffled the contents about until I came upon a picture. There he was. My Dad, holding a newly born me. His smile as wide as the bundle he carefully held. His eyes alive with the hopes of an endless sea of opportunities. I raced out to the office and enlarged the picture on the color copier until only a distorted set of eyes took over the page. The next morning, as the mechanic un-bolted the door, I shoved the paper in his face and said "THIS is the blue I want!"

The interior-detailer came to my office with a book of swatches.

"White." I said simply.

"But after finding the perfect shade of blue for the outside, don't you want to compliment the color with a certain hue of-"

I cut him off. "No. I told you I want white. Baby powder white. New-fallen snow white. I mean GHOST WHITE! Understand?"

After two weeks of anxiously waiting, it was time to pick her up. Now I would know what my father felt in his Vicky. My questions would be answered. Now I might better know my father.

When I walked into the garage, everyone in the shop stopped.

"That's one heck'uva beauty!" the mechanic gloated. "'Ya know how lucky 'ya are?"

I hadn't -- until just recently.

Vicky's V-8 beat strongly as I drove her home. I had breathed life into my Father's entombed dreams -- but I had found no solace. *I wish you knew how much I miss you, Dad.* I had done everything right. I followed the manuals, but my father was still gone. I sat in the driver's seat, defeated. I closed my eyes and thought back to the first time that I had laid eyes on Vicky. I had spent countless hours since then chasing his dreams, chasing him. If only he knew how much I loved him.

I had to take comfort in the notion that I found my Dad in the glow of the headlights, the chips of paint and the ashes of rust. I brought his dreams to life and resurrected lost memories. But he would never know.

I took the keys out of the ignition and threw them into the glovebox. Just then, a piece of paper fell out onto the floor. The yellowed paper was stained with oil and a bit crumpled. *Must be an old garage receipt.* I opened it up. All that it said was,

I Know.

Non-Fiction

East Main Street

Voices of Michigan

Cub Scouts and Other Oaths

Maralee Andree

Having grown up in a neighborhood where the only kids in uniforms we saw had just escaped from somewhere, I never knew much about Cub Scouting. And I didn't know anything about the Pinewood Derby.

The idea of the Pinewood Derby is for each Cub Scout and his dad to get together and build a little model car which then is raced when all the dens gather for the monthly pack meeting. The racing is not the important part, of course. The important part is the time spent together between the Cub Scout and his dad, time which will help cement the vital relationship between father and son that leads to a full and rewarding life when the youngster matures into an honest, hard-working, clear-eyed adult.

> **Maralee Andree** grew up in Sparta, Michigan. At the beginning of her junior year, Ms. Andree's family relocated to Rapid River, Michigan.

Apparently it works. The Cub Scouts have statistics to prove that no boy who participated in the Pinewood Derby ever grew up to be a chain saw murderer.

And so the first year our Cub Scout brings home his Pinewood Derby kit, we rush down to the basement where we spend an hour and a half together: five minutes reading the instructions, ten minutes sanding the wood, ten minutes spray painting the wood, ten minutes assembling the parts, ten

125

minutes re-reading the instructions, fifteen minutes taking off the wheels and putting them back on the right way, and thirty minutes arguing about which end is the front.

At the pack meeting that year, while I watch hopefully, our car finishes fourth out of six in our den. But on the way home, our Cub Scout says to me: "That's all right, I don't care if we didn't win. I still think you're the best dad in the world."

The second year our Cub Scout brings home his Pinewood Derby kit, we hurry down to the basement where we spend two hours together: thirty minutes sanding, fifteen minutes spray painting, fifteen minutes assembling, and an hour discussing why it's all right for a grown-up to say words "like that" when the electric sander slips and grinds all the hair off the back of his hand.

At the pack meeting that year, while I watch uncomfortably, our car finishes fifth out of six in our den. But on the way home, our Cub Scout says to me: "That's all right, I don't care if we didn't win. I still think you're a pretty good dad."

The third year our Cub Scout brings home his Pinewood Derby kit, we saunter down to the basement where we spend two and a half hours together: thirty minutes sanding, thirty minutes spray painting, thirty minutes assembling, and an hour explaining to the wife how it was possible to get red spray paint on the inside of her washing machine.

At the pack meeting that year, while I watch miserably, our car loses every race. And on the way home our Cub Scout says to me: "Boy, Keith sure is lucky. His dad never helps him with his car."

Despite my best efforts, our Cub Scout remains in the program and the next thing you know, I am a Den Leader. Becoming a Den Leader is not something you plan. It just sort of happens to you. Like hemorrhoids. One day you are spending your Tuesday evenings in front of the television set and the next thing you know you are standing there with two fingers in the air promising to do your duty. I'm not sure how it happened to me. I'm not even sure I want to think about it. All I know is that suddenly I am leader of Webelos Den 13, Pack 471.

Webelos are 10-year-olds making the transition from Cub Scouts to Boy Scouts. They are at that in-between stage. Too old to sit around the campfire with their mothers, but too young to care about where the Girl Scouts' showers are.

The first den meeting is held in our basement. It is attended by six Webelos. Before the next meeting, three of them will drop. Unfortunately, my kid is not one of them.

As suggested in the Webelo Leader's Book, we start the meeting with the Pledge of Allegiance to the Flag. More or less. The problem is, we don't actually have a flag, so we have to improvise. I'm not sure the national headquarters would approve of our substitute. On the other hand, there's nothing in the Webelo Leader's Book that says we CAN'T pledge allegiance to a Green Bay Packers' pennant.

In subsequent weeks, the meetings fall into a smooth routine: Open the meeting. Pledge Allegiance to the Green Bay Packers. Take attendance. Collect dues. Discuss a topic in the Webelo's Scout Book. Play a game. Eat cookies and drink Kool-aid. Adjourn the meeting. Let everyone out the front door. Let Tom back in the front door to get his hat. Let Tom out the front door. Let Brian back in the front door to get his Webelo's Book. Let Brian back out the front door. Let Joe back in the front door to get his brother. Let Joe and his brother back out the front door. Lock the front door. Disconnect the doorbell. Let the dog clean up the floor of its cookie crumbs.

After three months of this, I decide that what Den 13 needs is to take a field trip in lieu of one of its regular meetings. Not that the meetings are all that tough. But the doorknob is wearing out and the dog is getting awfully fat.

I bring up the subject during a Den meeting. "If you guys had your choice for a field trip, where would you like to go?"

"Hawaii."

"The Super Bowl."

"An X-rated movie."

I point out to the guy who suggested Hawaii that it would cost too much money to go there. I point out to the guy who suggests the Super Bowl that the game was played two months ago. I point out to the guy who suggests the X-rated movie that I wasn't really asking for suggestions from the other den leaders.

After considerable discussion, we narrow the field trip down to two choices: We can go on a tour of the local jail or visit the public library and see a slide show on the development and evolution of the Dewey Decimal System. We decided on the local jail.

On the eve of the Den's field trip, the other Den leader who had agreed to go along and help keep things under control calls to say that he will be unable to make it. An unexpected medical problem has cropped up. Not being suspicious by nature, I have no reason to doubt him. On the other hand, I have never heard of an emergency vasectomy.

The next day I pick up our Webelos after school and drive to the local jail. We arrive there at 3:48, which is quitting time. I know it is quitting time because just as we come in the front, I see a whole bunch of people hurrying out the back.

Inside, we are greeted by a man who says he will be our guide. He is not the regular guide, he adds, holding his short straw in a trembling hand. The regular guide called in a few minutes ago with an unexpected medical problem.

"Emergency vasectomy?" I ask.

"She didn't say."

We start our tour in the main office, where each Webelo is given a safety poster, suitable for framing or poking each other in the eyes. Then we tour the visitor's waiting room, where each Webelo is given a sample wanted poster. The poster is suitable for hanging, framing, or rolling up into swords. The guide, by this time, is asking for Valium.

We sword-fight our way through the kitchen, the laundry room, and into the booking office. In this room is the fingerprinting machine. The boys just love this gizmo. By the end of this part of the tour, I've got six Webelos not only fingerprinted but also now anxiously awaiting the tryouts for the next Disney Dalmatian Special. In this room, there are also assorted handcuffs, police sticks, and zappers. Hmmm... I wonder what kind of deal I could get on a set of six handcuffs.

The tour lasts 45 minutes. But it seems longer. We thank our guide, who by now is babbling and blinking uncontrollably, and head for the car.

"That was neat," one of the Webelos says.

"Yeah," another agrees. "Let's take another field trip again next week."

"Sorry, boys," I say. "I won't be able to take you."

"Why not?"

"I feel an unexpected medical problem cropping up."

Of course, scouting is more than pinewood derbies, den meetings and field trips to the local jail. Scouting is also packing up the old mess kit and hiking along forest trails with a song in your heart, a smile on your lips, and a thorn in your foot. Scouting is a camp-out in the woods.

My wife reminds me of our Cub Scout's annual camp-out.

"Sounds great," I say. "Sleeping under the stars. Waking up at the crack of dawn. Fishing in clear streams in the fresh pure air. Perhaps he'll see a raccoon. Some squirrels. A tiny little chipmunk."

"It's a father-son camp-out this year," she says.

"Of course you know there are bears in those woods. Big hairy man-eaters. And mountain lions. And gorillas. And sharks. And..."

"Are you trying to say you don't want to go?"

"Listen, if God intended man to sleep outside, why did he invent mosquitoes?"

"But if you don't go camping with your son, you'll break his heart. Besides it might be fun for you and I guarantee that you'll both develop a common interest."

"Yeah, we'll both learn to hate camping. So just forget it. I'm not going camping and I don't want to hear another word about it."

Wordlessly, she walks to the family room and begins

to make up the couch for me.   Wordlessly, I pack my knapsack.

That weekend we drive to Camp Hiawatha. Several other fathers and sons are already there when we arrive. One father is busy making a fire. I am somewhat surprised by this, seeing that it is in the middle of the afternoon and the temperature is in the 80s.

Another father has brought the two tents that we will call home for the next few nights. They are four-man tents, which is not to imply that four men can fit into them. A four-man tent is one that takes four men to put up. Fortunately, we have four men available. Unfortunately, they are the wrong four men. After half an hour of sweating, straining, fumbling, and Cub Scout oaths, we decide to read the directions.

Eventually the tents are up. It is time to begin the father-son activities. So we fish. We hike. We practice ax-handling skills. Before I know it, an hour has passed.

By nightfall, all the activities in the fresh forest air have worked their magic. Little heads begin to nod around the campfire. Tired little legs carry weary bodies to their sleeping bags before 10 o'clock. The kids, on the other hand, stay up all night.

The next morning we are up at the crack of dawn. Sunrise, I discover, looks just like sunset...only it's on the other side. We have breakfast: burnt pancakes, limp bacon, and shooting pains, prepared over a crackling propane stove.

Not long after breakfast comes the part I have been dreading. Taking one last breath of fresh forest air, I enter the building at the edge of the campsite. It is what they call a primitive facility, just like the pioneers used. After being in there for a few minutes, I begin to understand why the pioneers were always moving on.

The rest of the day is spent with more fishing, hiking, and ax-handling. In the afternoon, a Boy Scout comes along and shows us how to prepare our dinners so that they can be cooked directly on the hot coals of a campfire.

"Just wrap the foil real tight, put the food on the coals, and in fifteen or twenty minutes you'll have the best dinner you ever tasted," he assures us.

At 6 o'clock we place our tightly wrapped foil dinners on the hot coals of the campfire. At 6:05 it begins to rain.

As we sit in our tent, muddy, itchy and hungry, watching the best dinners we were ever going to taste sink into a pool of soggy ashes, my 10-year-old turns to me.

"Just think, Dad, this is my last year in Cub Scouts. We'll never get to do this again."

"Stiff upper lip, son."

"Yeah. Next year I'll be in Boy Scouts; then we get to come here for a whole week."

I wonder if there is anything in the Scout Leader's Book about it being okay for a scout to see a grown leader cry.

If nothing else, three years in Cub Scouts proves to be a learning experience. My scout now knows how to get wet every piece of clothing he has brought along five minutes after we arrive at a remote campsite, how to start a fire so that the smoke always blows into the tent, and how to tie a rope around his sleeping bag with a knot that won't come undone until we are in the car on the way home.

But there are some lessons I never seem to absorb.

When I hear the word "banquet," I still picture

elegantly dressed men and women being served Beef Wellington by white-gloved waiters. This all takes place in elegant surroundings, with gentle music playing in the background. Subdued lighting. Fine china. Expensive silverware. The Queen of England graciously hosting the elegant event. It is a fantasy that has survived approximately half a million Blue and Gold Banquets.

The Blue and Gold Banquet is a covered-dish event held each year to recognize the fact that the Pack has reached the point that is exactly halfway between the "Of Course I'll Volunteer To Help" stage and the "Oh No, Not Camp Time Again" stage. Then again, it could be merely a show of support for the Fried Chicken Workers of America, the Goulash Union, or the Teamsters For Better Jell-O.

At any given Blue and Gold Banquet, sixty out of a hundred covered dishes carried in will contain goulash. The rest will equally contain either chicken or Jell-O.

"One of these times I'm going to show up with a covered dish full of Beef Wellington and see what happens."

"You always were a troublemaker," my better half says. "Now let's get going before we're late. And don't forget the Jell-O."

We drive to the Colonel's, buy a bucket, transfer the chicken to our covered dish, and proceed to the banquet, which is being held in the Senior Citizens Center. It is not the elegant surroundings of my fantasy banquets. We arrive at the center and place our covered dish of chicken between the Goulash Surprise and the Shaved Carrot Jell-O Temptation.

When it is time for the banquet to begin, the

scoutmaster announces that we will go through the food line one den at a time. Our den will be last. We sit at our table, watching Scouts punch each other in the shoulder while the other dens go through the line. Finally, it is our turn. I carry my paper plate to the food table where I discover that the bowls of Jell-O are warm and the goulash is unrecognizable.

I pour myself a helping of Jell-O and poke through the remains of the chicken. I have my choice of two extra-soggy wings or a piece of bird that I do not recognize. I think it is a foot.

I put the two chicken wings into the pool of Jell-O and carry them back to the table. By the time I get there, the Jell-O has started to eat through the bottom of my plate. I stab at a wing with my plastic fork. Two of the three plastic tines snap off. With the remaining tine, I hold the chicken down while I saw at it with a plastic knife. The plastic knife cuts through the chicken, the liquid Jell-O, and the paper plate. Trying to ignore the green stain spreading out from underneath my plate, I eat the two chicken wings, pausing occasionally to cleanse my palate with warm Hawaiian Punch. The queen doesn't know what she's missing.

After three years of Blue and Gold Banquets, Pinewood Derbies, field trips, father-son campouts, and den meetings, our oldest son moves on to Boy Scouts. My sigh of relief is interrupted when our youngest son becomes a Cub Scout. Here we go again!

The Time We Invited Ann Sheridan

Philip J. Braun

It was April, 1940. George Spaulding and I walked down the halls at Flint Junior College. "Charlie" Trumbull spied us and called us into his office. I had a "D" in his accounting class and George, too, struggled with double-entry bookkeeping. We entered his office with trepidation.

"You two birds," Charlie said, "are the chairman and co-chairman of the spring dance. Dean Shattuck tells me I can have new basketball uniforms if there's any profit from the dance." Charlie glared at us. "I want those uniforms, gentlemen."

Charlie was also our basketball coach. He was a better basketball coach than he was an accounting instructor.

"You two handle the whole deal: sell tickets, crown a Queen, rent a hall, make a profit. I'll get you through accounting."

We were dismissed.

We sat down in the Men's Club Room and commiserated.

"What choice do we have?" I asked.

Philip Braun, a 78 year old resident of Flint, is a member of the Flint Writer's Club. A busy author, Philip is currently working on a collection of poetry, a novel and has completed a biography of Joseph Ryder, organizer of the Big Brothers in the Flint area.

135

"None," George answered. "It'll help me as a bench rider. Maybe he'll give me some playing time."

George came to my house after school. We needed a gimmick to help sell tickets.

"I have it," George said. "Let's write a letter to Ann Sheridan. (She was then the hottest star in Hollywood and I drooled when I saw her in a love scene on the silver screen.) We'll invite her to come to Flint and crown the Queen."

"She won't come," I said, starting to drool and seeing sexual images of her in a hot embrace, her body curvaceous, her hazel eyes sparkling, her white teeth shining. "Unless we make it a big deal, make it worth her while."

"Like giving her a new eight cylinder Buick Roadmaster?"

"Now you're talking."

"The car, a suite at the Durant Hotel, and the keys to the city."

"That ought to do it."

"I work at the News-Advertiser after school," George said. I'll bet the owner will let me put our letter on the front page. He'll think it's a gag."

"It'll sell tickets," I said.

"What about the car?" George asked.

"Why worry; she won't come. She's too busy, too popular."

We wrote the letter. It was on the first page of the paper. We put a copy on the school bulletin board and broadcast the news over our public address system.

We had a school contest and elected a Queen. We hired a hall and started to sell tickets. We took a lot of kidding from our friends who felt it was a joke.

Bob Mogford, another friend of mine at school, saw me in class a week after we mailed the letter. "Have you heard from Ann Sheridan yet?" he asked. I laughed and he laughed.

Later, I was asked to report to the Dean's office. A clerk handed me a letter addressed to George and me. It was postmarked Hollywood, California. I went looking for George.

We opened it.

Ann Sheridan, the raven-haired beauty, was coming to Flint. She would be pleased to crown the Queen, stay in a suite at the Durant, accept the keys to the city, and be presented with a new Roadmaster.

We had no car, no hotel suite, no keys to the city.

Visibly shaken, but ever-confident, George said, "Okay, so she's coming. We'll put her letter on the front page and publicize the hell out of this!"

There was the critical matter of the Roadmaster. We figured the suite and the mayor's office could wait. But the car?

I thought I had an answer.

My father was an old friend of William F. Hufstader, Sales Manager of Buick. He had been a guest in our home and was known as a genial gentleman.

I approached my father.

"Will you help us get an appointment with Mr. Hufstader? Will you go with us and explain our predicament?"

My father laughed heartily and said, "I'll see what I can do. You boys are in the soup and I want to see Bill

Hufstader stir it."

He got us our appointment.

We entered Mr. Hufstader's football-field size office at Buick. He grinned at my father and shook his hand and offered him a chair. His manner changed as he turned to us.

"What in the holy-hell do you two twerps think you're doing? Giving cars away? Who in the bloody-hell do you think you are to pull such a stunt?"

He went on before we could open our mouths.

"If Miss Sheridan comes to Flint, which I doubt very much, I will personally present her with a Roadmaster. You boys won't be any place in the picture. In return, you two get the dirtiest, filthiest, worst jobs at Buick I can find. You'll work your little butts off weekends and summers until that Roadmaster is paid for. Now, the both of you, get the hell out of my sight. I want to have a few words with Phil Senior. Don't slam the door on your way out."

We waited down on the street for my father. George said, "One down. Two to go. Let's get the suite and see the Mayor."

Then we had a jolt. E. L. Cross, our economics teacher, called us in his office. He had the front page of the News Advertiser featuring Ann Sheridan's response.

"You boys have been had," he said.

"What do you mean, sir?" George asked.

"Do you think a glamourous movie star is going to write you a personal letter? Do you see any letterhead showing a press agency or a movie studio? The letter is a fake."

138

He added, "Before you got it, did any of your pals ask
you whether you'd received a letter from Miss Sheridan? This
has all been arranged. Someone with a keen sense of humor
did this to you, and you birds fell for it."

"I'll bet it was Mogford," I said.

We chased Bob down. He broke out in a wide grin
and admitted his part and that of his girl friend. Jeanette
Rumbold (later to be his wife) had an aunt living in Los
Angeles. "I have an idea," Bob said to Jeanette.

They sat down and figured out a letter, as if written by
Ann Sheridan. They sent it to her aunt, telling her to mail it
back to JC, care of George Spaulding and Phil Braun, the
letter having a Hollywood postmark.

Bob and Jeanette kept their letter a secret and didn't
rat on us. They let us play out the scenario:

Tickets sold like mad. Peg Savage, our Queen, was
thrilled that Ann Sheridan would crown her. The manager
of the Durant, Scott Shattuck, after some harsh words,
obliged us with a suite. The mayor was delighted.

Two days before the dance, George and I received a
telegram. It was from Paramount Studios. Ann Sheridan was
ill and couldn't come to Flint. Her press agency was sending
roses to the Queen.

We faked the telegram and bought the roses. We got
through accounting. "Charlie" Trumbull got his basketball
uniforms.

Voices of Michigan

Scenes from a Classroom

Anne Beaty

I was an assistant in a special education classroom in Los Angeles. We had twelve seventh, eighth and ninth grade students in our room to whom we taught English, history, math and science. What we learned from each other, however, was something far less quantifiable.

Anne Beaty was born in New York and moved with her family to Rome, Italy when she was fourteen. Ms. Beaty has lived in California since 1970. She is self-educated and a single mother of a fifteen year old boy with whom she vacations each summer on Mackinac Island.

"Special" Ed

All children are (or should be) special to someone. All children deserve someone's undivided attention, at least some of the time. The teenager who's snarling at you, the girl with too much make-up, the boy with baggy pants are telling you something, asking you something, but sometimes it is very hard to hear. What they want, more than anything, is to be acknowledged, is to be told they are important, they are worthwhile, they matter.

There is a debate raging in education circles over the unproven merit of smaller class sizes. At least one oft-quoted study claims that there is no difference in standardized test scores between adolescents educated in groups of twenty or forty. What this debate misses are the incalculable benefits of the personal connections that can be forged between students

141

and teachers when there is sufficient time and space in the classroom.

The Spelling Lesson

He was a beautiful boy: small for his age, with sparkling deep black eyes and hair. There was a well of brilliance in him; he could grasp complexities and see relationships between disparate facts better than many adults. He was attending his third middle school in two years. Expelled for fighting, for weapon possession, for threatening a teacher, his file noted that he was a ward of his grandmother because his sixteen-year old mother had been crack addicted at his birth. He was as volatile as nitroglycerin.

I was new that semester. I was intimidated by these kids - by their colors, their experiences, their backgrounds which were so different from mine; but most of all, I was appalled by their ignorance. So I raided the text-book room for a stack of spelling workbooks, in every grade level from two to nine, and I began testing each student to find where to begin.

In the meantime, the administrative powers-that-be had decreed that this was the year for teachers to be "stulled." Being "stulled" meant that at any moment an administrator would sit down in the room and observe, for a minute, an hour or a day, and then write a critique on the teacher. We were supposed to have "lesson plans" which we should follow verbatim, specific files, targets of achievement, and bulletin boards with standards of behavior and consequences listed, plus numerous other requirements. We were also supposed to be trying to teach these kids something.

So, here we were, an hour or two into the day. I had six kids at a table in the back of the room, working over the spelling books.

"Carlos, please don't draw in the book, we have to give them back; no Maria, Jenny can't tell you how to spell *there*, I need to know what YOU know; Luis, please sit down; Carlos, please don't draw on the table; hello, Jose, are you awake? Jenny, lipstick belongs in the bathroom; WELL DONE, Miguel, you need a harder book; Carlos, please stop drawing on Jenny."

The door opened and in walked an administrator. The boy leaped to his feet, jumped over the table (scattering students and books), flung himself at her and shouted, "I'm in ninth grade spelling, isn't that incredible!!" The administrator hugged him, and over his head, mouthed to the teacher, "You pass," and left the room.

United Colors

It's spring, and it's been a long, hot, stressful day. I have gone to a table by the open window with three students in an advanced history group, but our quiet work has attracted two others who are sitting and listening. Our lesson includes no racial issues, but even before the Rodney King incident, if you are young, poor and black or brown in Los Angeles, everything has to do with race, and so we are discussing prejudice. In a pause in the conversation, I look down at the table, and look again, and say,

"Nobody move."

They freeze.

"Look at our arms."

They look down, look up at me, look at each other.

"Look, you guys, look at the color of our skin."

Now they begin to see what I suddenly saw. I'm a fair-skinned white, who happens to have a pretty good tan this year, among two blacks and three Hispanics, and no one could possibly guess who is who by the colors on those arms. My arm is darker than all but one, an Hispanic arm, and another is as fair as any Aryan's. We study this, in near silence, until the bell rings.

The Gardener's Son

He appeared in the classroom two months into the semester. He was Hispanic. His English was fluent but accented. He was quiet, sitting in the front row and working hard at whatever assignment he was given. In fact, he was so diligent that, I confess, we kind of lost sight of him in the uproar that was our normal classroom environment. Oh, his grades were recorded, his work was praised, he was used as a buffer between more obstreperous students, but we didn't really look closely at him until he'd been with us more than a month. I suddenly realized that he was reading at his grade level, his math skills were solid, he clearly did not have a behavior program, so why was he in a special ed class? Some judicious questioning elicited the information that his father was a gardener, and he had come to us from the richest and whitest school district in Southern California. We tested him that same day, and he transferred to regular classes the next week. The last I heard, he was a sophomore at California State University.

José

In seventh grade, when I first met him, he was the kind of boy you just wanted to hug - round and twinkling, a teddy-bear of a boy. He wasn't the smartest kid, but he was (usually) willing to try, and so good-natured about his deficits that everyone who knew him was always available to help him a little more. By eighth grade, the pull of the gangs was stronger, and although he was still sweet and willing when he was at

144

school, outside the gates life was getting rough and dangerous. His father was in state prison for homicide, his uncle was a gang leader, and we never heard much about his mother. At the beginning of ninth grade, he was expelled for bringing a knife to school, and I knew he was lost to us. All this was seven years ago, but I never forgot him.

Last year, I'm told, during the lunch hour, a handsome young man walked into the classroom. As the teachers greeted him with cries and hugs and exclamations, he told his story. At a continuation school, he had a girlfriend from the regular school, a cheerleader no less. At first, her parents had disapproved, but as he stayed in school, and they stayed together, her parents came to like him. After a year, when his family fell completely apart, they invited him to live with them. As he told this, he said, "And they sat down and ate dinner at the table every night, all of them. I never knew anyone who did that." He's in college now, and they are still together.

Tardy Policy

He was not a student I had much affection for. He was quiet and immature. I gravitated toward the loud, aggressive problem children. He was a good student, however, except that he arrived 15 minutes late, day after day after day. We chastised him, and marked him "tardy," and let it go at that. Until one day I began to wonder.

"James, why are you late to school every day?"

"Well, I don't wake up in time."

"How come? You could get up earlier and be here by 7:55."

"Yes, OK, I'll try."

The weeks rolled by and the tardy marks continued.

"James, you're still tardy every day."

"Well, I don't wake up in time."

"What could you do to get yourself here on time?"

"I just have to get up earlier."

For once, the other students were working quietly, and my curiosity was piqued.

"What time do you set your alarm for?"

"I don't gots no alarm."

"Oh. Well, what time does your mom wake you up?"

"She don't wake me, she's gone."

"Oh. What about your dad?"

"He's gone too."

After an hour of careful questioning, I had the whole story. Dad worked nights, and didn't get home until 9 a.m. Mom left for work at 5 a.m. James had to rouse, feed and dress his three younger siblings, drop the little one off at the baby-sitter as he walked the other two to their elementary school, and then get to school himself. There was not one clock in their one-bedroom apartment.

That evening, I walked through my house counting our timepieces. I came up with 14. Try it: the clocks on the microwave, the stove, the VCR. The timers on the thermostat, the decorative clocks in the living room and den, the dress watch, the every-day watch, the watch no one ever wears, the alarm clocks by every bed, the travel clocks in a drawer.

I asked him, "If you had an alarm clock, what kind would it be: a plug-in one, or a wind-up one?" Then I went to a drug store and for $3.99 bought him a large, old-fashioned wind-up alarm clock, and showed him how to set it.

He was never late to school again.

Culture Wars

Bob was the loudest kid I ever met. He was smart and

swaggering, with the loudest, filthiest mouth in school. You could hear him coming half a block away, and every second word was x-rated. But he was a marshmallow. He cared about his work, wanted you to like and approve of him. He blossomed under praise and wilted under criticism. He had been in special classes since fourth grade. His volume was certainly disruptive, and he was incapable of not calling out the door to any acquaintance who happened to be passing by, but other than this, I couldn't quite see why he was in special ed. His ability to learn was surely no less developed than that of the "regular" students.

Over two years, we devised many strategies to deal with his disruptions, none of which were particularly effective. We tried to keep the classroom door closed, but the windows were open, so the shouting to his friends continued. We teased him and penalized him for his language; it became a classroom joke how many pieces of trash Bob would have to pick up at the end of the period. He took it all in good humor, and oh, he tried. I watched his struggle with pity in my heart, and watched him lose his battle every day. Then, two things occurred that opened my eyes.

I happened to come across an article about black students at an Ivy League college. The writer mentioned that in the black culture, it is considered beyond the pale to pass by another black student without acknowledging them, with a back-slap or a high five or a "hey bro!" And then, on the evening of open house, where parents are invited to meet their children's teachers, as we sat in our quiet classroom, we heard from far away, a woman's voice bellowing. As she came closer (and louder), we looked at one another in sudden understanding. Every other word was x-rated, and the volume was stuck on "high." She appeared in our doorway. Bob's

147

mother had come to thank her son's teachers for "putting up with him."

I never got a clear answer as to why Bob was in special ed. Would his behavior have been considered so "disruptive" in a school system not run by whites? What did we really teach him, other than that his culture was unacceptable? Fortunately, we never did manage to teach him that.

Teaching Math

At my son's private school, arithmetic is taught through creative games the children play with one another, using special sets of cards and colored tokens. They find it so enjoyable it becomes a favorite free-time activity, and by the time "real" math starts in fourth grade, they are well-prepared. But what do you do with 12 adolescents, some of whom can't subtract with borrowing, some who still add on their fingers, and some who think they know fractions, but don't know their 3Xs tables.

In the midst of all the talk about "Old Math," "New Math" and "New New Math," in the clamor for raising test scores and higher achievement tests and quantifiable results, I decided to start at the beginning. I made a chart with every math function I could think of across the top, and the student's names down the side. The skills began with adding whole numbers, progressed through subtraction, multipli-cation, division, moved through the same sequence with fractions and then decimals, and ended with percents and the beginnings of algebra. I bought stickers, and made up packets of worksheets to cover every line of my chart. I told them they could not move to the next line until they had fully demonstrated mastery of the previous one. I offered a free lunch of their choice to any student who memorized the times tables to 12, and a calculator to any student who passed long division. In other words, I became a benevolent despot.

Oh, did they kick and scream. "The other class gets to use calculators!" "This is SOOOO boring." "Why do I have to do another sheet of subtraction, I KNOW this." They moaned and they groaned and they whined, and the stickers started to go up, and someone got a pizza, and someone else got a new calculator to keep, and the pencils wore out and I got in trouble for over-use of the Xerox machine. That year, four of my students joined "regular ed" math classes. The teacher told me they were better prepared than 80% of the others.

Algebra and geometry have their place in the world, but you can't balance a checkbook without subtraction, you can't calculate a tip without knowing percentages, and you can't use a calculator for division if you don't understand division because you'll enter the wrong number first. If you can't figure out the price of three movie tickets plus popcorn, you won't know how much money to beg from your parents.

The Dance of the Lemons

When my son entered first grade at our local public school, I asked if I could assist in the special ed class across the hall. I was not yet an employee of the school district, but I was interested in working with special needs children.

The class consisted of a wonderful, enthusiastic teacher, her male assistant, and eight retarded children, ages seven to ten. The four children with Down Syndrome had the additional speech deficits and vision programs that often go along with Down. One boy was classified autistic and hyperactive. One girl had been brain-damaged at birth.

I was fascinated by the children, and happy to do any task the teacher gave me. But as the months went by, I couldn't help noticing that the assistant did as little as possible, argued with the teacher over virtually everything, and treated the kids as if they were untrained puppies. He was never cruel, but always dismissive. Then, one day when we were watching them play during recess, he finally expressed himself to me.

"All this education is nonsense!" he said. "None of them will ever learn anything. They're possessed by the devil, and that's that." I was so stunned, I could only walk away.

Many months later, when I went to the principal of that school for a recommendation for my employment application, I told her this story, and asked why they kept him in a position for which he was so clearly unsuited. From her desk, she picked up a lemon that had four toothpicks stuck in it to resemble arms and legs. Without saying a word, she danced that lemon across her desk. When I questioned her with my puzzled look, she explained.

"It's the dance of the lemon. We inherited him from another school, not knowing what he was like, and soon we'll send him on to yet another school, and we'll be able to hire someone more suited to that class." She laughed, and set the lemon back in its place.

The lemons are still dancing through the system, and the only losers are the children in their classes.

An Instinct for Grief

Bonnie Flaig

Within minutes after baby pigs are born, they push themselves to their feet and begin a hyperkinetic movement. They shimmy and shake like religious zealots. Their fresh hides gleam from the slime of the birth sack. This dance is part of their amazing instinct to preserve their own life: they are whipping themselves into existence, like those watches you shake to start them running. Time is crucial for newborn pigs. They need to find food, and the ecstatic movement of the piglets near the mother's nipples encourages milk production to begin.

Bonnie Flaig teaches English full-time at Kalamazoo Valley Community College. She has had several poems published in small literary magazines and is on a lifelong mission to fit more writing time into her life.

What I know of pigs I learned during Christmas, 1993, while visiting my in-laws' farm near Greenleafton, Minnesota. My husband and I were the only ones still up the night before Christmas Eve. I was exhausted and wanted to go to bed, but Mike, nostalgic for his past on the farm, accepted the unspoken responsibility of being the last male awake that night. He was worried about a sow who was ready to "come in" on this cold night and left the house to check on her. Five minutes later he was back in the doorway. I had been dozing in an easy chair, not listening to Jay Leno.

"Want to see some pigs being born?"

His face was red, moustache covered with white frost melting to water droplets.

"Why not?" And I began the laborious task of dressing for subzero temperatures.

The barn smelled like hay, warm breath, and pig manure. It was quiet as a church. Mike left most of the lights off. We walked over to the fourth metal crate along the wall. A sow lay inside, heaving like a big, dirty inner-tube. Four tiny piglets worked at her nipples, and while I watched she rolled backwards slightly.

"She's exposing her udder for the ones already born," Mike explained.

He lifted the top of a wooden box near the crate to show me two even newer piglets squirming damp under a heat lamp.

"It's so cold," he said, "so as soon as they're born I put them in here to dry off a bit and wake up."

He closed the lid and a few minutes later we heard bumping. The pigs were jumping in the heat box and knocking their heads against the top. They were ready and eager to join the others.

The farm is a tranquil, slower paced haven from the demands of our urban world. I love to visit here. Mike also seems to enjoy the chance to get away from the employee and customer complaints he encounters in his job and muck around on the farm for a few days. Farm life is intriguing and a bit foreign to me, even though my family owns a farm in Redwood County, Minnesota. I lived on that farm for just seven years as a child in the 1960's. I was the fourth of five children. Back then, it seemed to me the idea was to leave the farm. My parents worked hard so that all five children could go to college and have a life away from farming, which is what we all did. In 1969 my parents left the farm, too, because my father found farming a lonely profession. Still, though he no longer farmed himself, he continued to work with farmers at the county ASCS office until his death. He would have been amused, maybe pleased, to see me standing at this sow crate in the early hours of a Christmas Eve morning, rubbing my hands together to keep my fingers warm.

My father died suddenly on a Saturday evening in October, 1987. He had spent that day chopping wood and attending the wake and funeral of an old high school teacher. Apparently the teacher had been strict, but someone he admired. He joked with a friend later that day about attending the teacher's wake. "I swear she still had one eye open watching me."

In a perfect world, grief should bring people together, but in my family it didn't. Our shared memories of Dad--the Brut aftershave, Doublemint gum, his humor, love of the Catholic church and anything Irish--should have made us try harder to maintain our connection with each other. But instead our individual pain sent us off spinning in different directions. For reasons I still don't understand, our grief was edged with petty criticism of each other.

We even seemed to disagree on how to remember Dad. For instance, most of my siblings would probably tell about my father attending that teacher's funeral on his last day in reverent tones, as an example of my father's character. How he seldom missed a chance to show his respect by attending funerals of old chums and distant relatives. But I can't tell the story without including the joke about the eye.

By Christmas last year, two of my sisters announced they would not be spending Christmas with the family, leaving the rest of us with sort of a "why bother?" attitude. Mom philosophized. "You're all adults now with spouses of your own. Maybe you shouldn't feel the obligation to get together at Christmas." Things looked the same this Christmas. We had no plans for a family gathering.

Mike was anxious because it had been awhile since any pigs had been born. He picked up a bar of soap floating in a bucket of warm water he'd brought from the house and began to scrub his right arm. Then he went inside the sow to check whether any piglets were caught in the birth canal. I took a step back. I felt like a child staring at something I shouldn't see as his forearm and elbow disappeared inside her.

"There's more up in the womb," he said.

"So what do we do?"

"Wait."

The barn was dark except for the heat lamp. Occasionally I would see a pair of eyes flash across from me. Then a cat or two would jump up and slink along the sow's crate and the empty one next door, circle, and come back. The cats feigned a leisurely attitude while their glance slid downward at the steaming piglets. They didn't want to be caught staring at what they desired. I learned later that a hungry cat will eat a piglet if he can get hold of one, especially in a cold winter. Cats are not the money-making animals on this farm, so feeding them is sometimes forgotten. When I learned that cats caught eating baby pigs might be shot by my father-in-law, I made it my business to bring dry cat food to the barn for the rest of the week.

Mike and I stayed quiet. It wasn't good to distract the sow from what she needed to do to finish this birth. Sometimes her fitful panting would subside and she would appear to sleep briefly. She was old, Mike told me. She had given birth so many times that I wondered if she dreamed of labor, of an endless stream of piglets sliding from her. One of nature's tricks, or blessings, is that many animals, pigs at least, don't recognize their own kin. Mike told me that if one sow gave birth to an extra large litter while another had a small litter, piglets could be moved from the large litter to the small one just to even things out. Neither mother would mind. Next summer, as this sow watched from the outdoor pen waiting to be bred yet again, she would not recognize any of those struggling fat hogs being loaded into the old red trailer as her own.

The sow birthed an amazing fourteen piglets that night. Two were runts. "Genetically inferior," Mike said, but I found this hard to believe since the runts looked perfect in every way but size. They stayed in the wooden box under the heat lamp all night. Mike brought me a syringe and filled it by tugging and squeezing one of the sow's teats until a stream of white milk shot out. I watched him feed one runt. With his large index finger he coaxed the tiny mouth open and dropped in a little milk. He spoke so gently to the pig, as if talking to a baby. Then it was my turn to feed the other runt. At first, its tiny perfection and opaque skin were mildly revolting to me. But as I cradled him in the crook of my elbow and coaxed him to take a few drops of milk, my feelings changed. Surely they could make it, with the help of the heat lamp, the syringe, and me. After all, Fern saved Wilbur!

155

We finally went to bed at about 3:00 a.m. When we returned at 8:00, the smaller runt was dead. I buried my grief by pinning all my hopes on the other, which I thought was looking perkier today.

I put him in with his litter mates. He held his own, shimmying like the others and trying to claim one of his mother's nipples. But he was too short to reach even the lowest nipples as she lay on her side. He was small and entirely pink while the others were marked with black spots and bands, a small bloody stump on each rear end from the routine tail-clipping. My little runt still had his tail, and he tried to keep up with his siblings, following as they darted en masse from one side of the crate to the other. I was amused by the lack of individuality: all the pigs ran one way, then the other, or they all slept, or they all tried to eat. Activities changed quickly and there was almost an urgency to stay part of the group. The runt was always a few steps behind the others. He was often knocked down, and soon his little foot was bleeding from where it had gotten stuck in the grate. His tiny trail of blood mingled with that of the others' tails. Finally, the runt managed to climb on top of one of his sleeping brothers for warmth and fell into a peaceful, short sleep. There was more shuffling, he slid, and then he was nestled between two of his huge mates.

I carried this last mental picture back into the house and helped my mother-in-law with Christmas preparations. I wrapped a few gifts, decorated sugar cookies with pink and green frosting. I made Pizza Popovers, a recipe from the local church cookbook, for the noon meal. I was tired from the barn vigil of the night before, so in the afternoon I took a long nap.

Before supper I bundled up once again and walked out to the barn where Mike, his brother, and father had been working most of the day. I could hear their voices but couldn't find them when I entered the barn. I walked over to the sow crate. She was lying absolutely still while piglets sucked at her nipples. Her eyes moved up to meet mine. I reached over the bar to scratch her spine.

The runt was not with the others, and somehow I knew where to look. Under the crate ran a trough used for cleaning the barn. There, in the dark sludge and manure, lay the pink piglet. I squatted to get a closer look. His eyes were closed, mouth open.

"I didn't want you to see him," Mike said, walking up behind me.

"It's O.K.," I said. I was cool. I tried to adopt the stoicism that I had seen farmers display regarding the life and death of animals. Inside, I was devastated. My mind was flailing about for something positive in this experience, something to halt the approaching despair. After all, it was Christmas.

With effort, I conjured the image of those few moments when the runt pig slept peacefully between his brothers, grateful for the simple comfort that brief memory gave me.

Back in the house I said hello to my sisters-in-law and Mike's nieces and nephews who had arrived and gathered in the kitchen. Later we would all sit down to oyster stew and lefse rolled with butter and brown sugar.

I sneaked upstairs to the room where we slept and closed the door.

It was Christmas Eve.

I sat on the bed and cried.

157

Voices of Michigan

Seascapes:
A Compilation of Essays

Constance Baker

Remembering

My playground was the sand dunes of the North Carolina Coast, her beaches and the mighty Atlantic Ocean. My playmates, her many treasures.

Constance Baker is a 73 year old - young senior transplanted from the Carolina ocean to Michigan's lakes. Through her Carolina years, she wrote to entertain abused children. She has had *A Bench in the Park* published.

I remember . . . the searing heat of the sun's rays as it beat on my skinny limbs . . . the burning sands shifting beneath bare feet . . . the cool dampness felt when digging wells that playful waves soon filled.

I remember . . . stiff breezes wafting the odorous scent of drying fish beached by stormy tides, so repulsive to "inlanders" but meaning home to me . . . the salty taste of sun-chapped lips . . . refreshing cold water trickling down a parched throat.

I remember . . . searching through damp sand for clams that disappeared immediately with only a bubble marking their passage.

I remember . . . hunting flat, white sand dollars and domed-shaped sea urchins . . . the excitement of finding the elusive star fish . . . harvesting soggy sponges that dried so drab and hard but retained a sea-weedy fragrance . . . scraped knees and toes from jagged coral.

I remember . . . breathlessly watching diminutive ghost crabs venture forth at twilight. Jet-black eyes would appear outside their hole, like tiny periscopes. On some mysterious signal out popped a ghostly head . . . then claws. They scuddered along with a sidewise crawl. One could not help laughing at their struggle to fit large morsels of food through impossible small doors!

I remember . . . striving to identify the water birds: terns, tall-legged cranes, herons and sandpipers. My tattered dog-eared book was stained from dirty fingers, peanut butter and sea spray. It was crusty with salt and scratched almost unreadable from gritty sand. It was my most treasured possession.

I remember . . . brown pelicans fishing along the shore. Graceful dolphins dancing beyond breaking waves, dripping water sparkling like many jeweled diamonds on their coal black fins.

I remember . . . thrilling to an instant picnic. Gulls clutching clams or oysters, flying high and letting them crash down upon the road . . what a can opener!

I remember . . . how funny it was to see the gulls picking meat from broken shells, while hopping around on the hot pavement to avoid sticky, tarry blisters. Unsuspecting drivers were startled into dodging these flying missiles or the sound of shattering windshields and popping tires mingled with pounding surf!

I remember . . . one early morning, standing on a lofty dune. I gazed out over a calm sea. A mild, southerly wind was blowing. A small herd of wild "banker" ponies trotted fearlessly into the ebb tide. They were headed for a favorite feeding ground. The stallion carefully pointed the herd of mixed mares and colts. Careless mares that strayed toward the open sea were turned from certain death by a sharp nip on the flank.

I remember . . . the ocean's angry waves, pounding the dunes with a deafening roar like hundreds of runaway freight trains. The howling winds and the sudden silences made me tremble for the sailors caught out on such dangerous seas. Goose pimples danced on my skin. My hair would stand straight up, as if pulled by some magical hand. Lightning cracked!

I remember . . . calm seas murmuring lullabies.

Yes . . . I remember!

Sea Child

I'm home-sick - not for people but for my country. Come take a walk with me, friend. My heart needs to share memories. God and you only, will understand.

To describe my growing up in the low country of the North Carolina outer banks, friend, I will have to take you to the marsh on a spring day, flush the great blue heron from its silent occupation, scatter marsh hens as we sink to our knees in mud. Open you an oyster with a pocket knife and feed it to you from the shell and say, "There, that taste, that's the taste of my childhood." I would say, "Breathe deeply," and you would breathe and remember that smell for the rest of your life. The bold, fecund aroma of the total marsh, exquisite and sensual, the smell of the South in heat. A smell like new milk, semen, and spilled wine, all perfumed with sea water. My soul grazes like a lamb on the beauty of indrawn tides.

Then we take a long hike along the lonely beaches of the Atlantic feeling the heat from the burning sun on our faces, while we watch the rolling waves build up far out of the deep, blue waters. We watch the color turn emerald green nearer the shore, changing to gray as they break against the beach. We laugh together as the waves dip their white caps to us in the joy of freedom as they swirl in brown foam around our bare feet. We feel the pull of the outgoing tide as we sink our toes deeper into the sand till we have no feet at all and tumble onto the cool damp sand in the gladness of abandonment!

Can't you feel the coolness of the salt spray on your face, making your shirt stiff across your shoulders? Friend, breathe deep of the damp warm sea air . . . It carries the perfume of the growing plants of the islands. My islands, though no one ever owns an island. They belong to the sea, their mother. The islands move to her rhythm, forever changing, always dying and being reborn. Dune sand flies through the air with the restless winds! Do you not feel the sting on your bare skin? It is like red hot needles!

Stop a moment with me, my friend, along this deserted strip of beach. What's that? Did I say deserted? See the restless retreating wave? Watch the sand. What is making those air bubbles? Dig swiftly, my friend. See the little clams hurrying back to the safety of the sea? Look at the big black eyes of the ghost crab. Look oceanward just beyond the breakers. It's a school of dolphins breaking water. Watch them play, the sun gleaming on their dark wet bodies. See the flight of the pelicans skimming the breakers? Oh! That one just dove into the waves. There, see the fish hanging from his pouch? He's going to lose it - no, he swallowed the fish! Yes, I saw you slip a sand dollar in your pocket. Be careful, it is so fragile, it is easily broken. A lovely treasure of the deep.

Twilight is falling on our long southern evening and suddenly the full moon has lifted its forehead of stunning gold above the horizon - lifted straight out of the filigreed light, intoxicated clouds that lay on the skyline in attendant veils. See, behind us the sun is setting in simultaneous congruent withdrawal as the sea turns to flame in a quiet duel of gold . . . the new moon, astonishing and ascendant, and the depleted gold of sunset extinguishing itself in the long westward slide. It is the old dance of days in the Carolina marshes, the breathtaking death of days until the sun vanishes, its final signature - a ribbon of bullion strung across the tops of sea-oats, gracefully dancing along the dunes. The moon is rising quickly now, like a bird from the waters making a silhouette of the islands. See, it climbs straight up, golden orange, then gold, then yellow, then pale yellow, pale silver, silver-bright, then something miraculous, immaculate and beyond silver, a color native only to southern nights.

Look out to sea. The fishing boats, all lit, arriving home with the evening catch of shrimp. Hear the calls of the sea gulls following the fishing fleet begging for a treat? See the bobbing lights of the fishermen's lanterns - the shapes of flounders inlaid in sand like the silhouettes of ladies in cameos.

Look upward, see millions of brilliant stars. God has lighted His windows again tonight. The air is so clear, the stars so close, let's pick a few! Remember the childhood nursery rhyme?

163

Twinkle, twinkle little star
How I wonder what you are
Up above the world so high
Like a diamond in the sky.

Star light, star bright
First star I've seen tonight
I wish I may, I wish I might
Have the wish I wish tonight

I'm so very glad God, You shared all this beauty with me all through the years of my childhood.

Listen . . listen to the soft sound of the lapping waves . . . a night time lullaby so very beautiful! Stretch out on the hot, warm sand. Move your hips and shoulders to make a cup. Are you comfortable? Lie back and gaze at wonders above you. Tune your ears to the night sounds! Feel the softness of the sea breeze. Relax. Drift. Dream.

Awaken to the feel of dew on your closed eyelids. A new day is being born. Wake up, become one with the miracle. The soft hues of pink splash across the new morning. A Master Painter must have spilled His bucket. See how the colors drip over the edges of heavy, white clouds? There! A splash of gold over all, as the sun peeks over the horizon.

Have you ever thought on the mystery of why both the rising and setting sun seem to return to the sea? Why the moon is born of the sea?

I am a child of the sea. Someday, I shall return to her - in death.

Carp in the Pool

Rita Walsh

The summer of 1962 does not stand out as a particularly eventful year in my childhood. The Beatles had captured the heart of every young girl, including mine. The fantasy that somehow George or Ringo would spot me in a crowd and whisk me away to live happily ever after consumed most of my free time. Other than that, I cannot bring to mind any major events.

There is, however, a rather murky recollection of a fiasco involving my brother and another neighborhood rascal.

I recount this episode not as a spectator but on second-hand information gathered from my brother and mother.

My brother, Ed, as the family still calls him even though his given name is Angelo, spent a lot of time cooking up interesting things to do with his neighborhood friend, Bob.

Bob will be forever imprinted on my mind, racing down the street on his red and white coaster bike complete with large wire basket in front. He used his bike to deliver papers. At that time paper routes were for "real men." Men who could daily brave the elements in the early hours of the morning. Men who could fold and throw and still balance on

Rita Walsh lives in Auburn Hills with her husband and two sons. Presently she works part-time for an interior designer. Mrs. Walsh has written one other short story about the Detroit News-paper strike that was published in a small union newsletter.

two wheels. A smile creeps over my lips whenever a bicycle like Bob's crosses my path.

I find myself using that old cliche, "Things were different when I was a girl." The same phrase that makes my kids cringe with fear that I'm going to tell yet another story about how things used to be. Well, things **were** different. Mothers were free from worry as their kids roamed the neighborhood amusing themselves. Boarding the bus for a downtown Detroit shopping spree was a tradition, as was riding our bikes down to Lake St. Clair in search of relief from the scorching summer heat. The pavement radiated heat during those summer months that seemed to stretch into eternity. The northeast side of Detroit might as well have been the Sahara Desert.

The lake's cool breezes beckoned to anyone who could stand the steamy half-hour bike ride rubbing elbows with the traffic down Moross Road. Ed and Bob often braved that ride not only in pursuit of relief from the heat, but the prospect of reeling in large fish drew them to the blue-green waters of the lake. Mischief rode at their heels each time those two embarked on a seemingly harmless pastime, and this day was no different.

Swimming and fishing were prohibited off Lake Shore Drive, in the affluent suburb of Grosse Pointe, but that certainly was not a deterrent for this dynamic duo. By age twelve they had mastered the routine of avoiding the law.

This part I know first hand, for it was these two who taught me how to ride a bike nonchalantly on Lake Shore Drive, wait for a lull in the traffic, and then make a mad dash to the water's edge. Then we would throw our bikes over the break wall onto the large boulders that framed the coastline setting them down as close to the break wall as possible so as not to be seen from the street and police cars that patrolled the area. The next step was to lay down in a line on the ledge that ran along the break wall about two feet below ground level on the water's side providing the perfect hiding place for us kids.

Only after peeking over the grassy ledge and being sure that the coast was clear, would we climb down onto the boulders and enjoy the marvelously cool water. Fishing poles would be rigged up and lines cast into the thrashing waves. Heads had to be kept low and a sharp eye kept open for the law. At any sign of a possible police car, all jumped back on the ledge and lay quietly until they passed, hopefully unnoticed.

Ahhhh, those were the days of childhood. Little did my mom know what went on during these fishing trips or she would never have allowed it. Ed and Bob were stopped by the police at times and even fined once or twice, but that did not dampen their spirit. They were fearless, and desperate for something to do, and this was just the thing to satisfy their taste for harmless adventure.

Having been victorious that day in the struggle of man-versus-fish, Ed and Bob rode home with their prize, a two-foot carp. Knowing that this was not choice eating, the boys were left with the dilemma of what to do with their catch. A hardy fish, it was still alive, though just barely. They decided that it belonged back in water. Where could they find water, several miles from the lake? Gary's pool!

Gary lived across the street and was one of those kids who for some reason had a hard time getting along with others. Whether kids picked on him or he picked on them, I don't know, but anyway there was animosity.

Gary's mom was a meticulously neat and clean woman with a well-groomed yard, along with a properly maintained pool. Kids like Ed and Bob were seldom invited to sample the cool waters of that pool, and. looking back now, I can understand why. They placed the sizeable carp in the pool. There it was, swimming slowly on its side, using the last shred of life left in its body. With a long black rope-like streamer trailing from its bottom, its silvery skin gleamed in the bright summer sun in the crystal-clear chlorine water. Streamers that had already been excreted were floating gently. Its saucer-like eyes were staring, its mouth opening and closing, opening and closing, gasping its last breath.

I don't recall Gary's mom having a hot tempered nature, but this would make even the meekest of people red in the face. How she came to the conclusion that Bob was behind this, I never knew. Nonetheless, she had words with Bob's mother and, of course, Bob implicated Ed.

That brought the whole sordid matter to our house, Bob and his mom, in a not-so-pleasant state of mind.

My mom usually went about her daily chores with an English-Italian dictionary close at hand, as her use of the English language was almost non-existent at that time. So when the knock came at the door and the dilemma of how to handle this presented itself, she ran for her book, a gift from none other than Bob.

Of course Bob's mother presumed him innocent and proceeded to defend him as my mom listened. My brother acted as the interpreter. My mother, being a shrewd judge of character, listened to the jumbled "he said, she said" details and discerned that both boys were probably equally guilty.

Finally my brother confessed and implicated Bob as his co-conspirator. My mother appealed to Bob's conscience. She relayed to my brother in Italian to have Bob look her in the eye and tell her the truth. As Ed did so in English, Bob slowly hung his head and admitted his guilt.

There was still a now-dead carp to be fished out of the pool and disposed of. The pool had to be drained and cleaned for the second time. This was not the first time that a dead fish had been found in that pool. To this day it remains a mystery as to who was responsible for the first one, but I'm sure Ed and Bob know the answer.

There was never any love lost between Bob's family and ours over this incident. Bob and Ed went on to perpetrate many such crimes. They remained friends throughout their childhood. In high school, they drifted their own ways and then into adulthood. Even though they haven't seen each other in many years, I know that they both cherish these memories.

At family gatherings we are still getting a good laugh over the carp incident. I'm sure that Bob's kids have heard this story and probably cringe whenever he starts with, "when I was your age."

Voices of Michigan

170

Shore Leave

Marion E. Boyer

It is midnight. I wait in the warm sand and listen to the rush-hush of waves. A great prehistoric creature emerges dripping from the Atlantic, hauls itself from the shallow surge of water onto the beach moving as inexorably as evolution. The sea turtle pulls her weight to reach a point high above the tideline. A deep trail like tractor tracks marks her progress. She is here to lay her eggs.

I am here with women friends sharing a rented condo. We are all mothers escaping for a week-long holiday together in Florida. A twenty-six mile strip of this shoreline near Melbourne, Florida, is a preserve for endangered sea turtles to nest undisturbed. Nearby condominium residents are required to shade their evening lights. Dogs are prohibited on the beach unless leashed. The turtles nest at night and over a season more than ten thousand nests are usually recorded by the patrolling rangers. This July night my two friends and I alone witness one turtle's labors.

> **Marion E. Boyer** is a full-time teacher of communication courses at Kalamazoo Valley Community College. An outdoor enthusiast, Marion has had several essays published in *Paddler, Canoe and Kayak*, and *American Whitewater Magazine*, and poetry published in *Driftwood Review, Standing Wave*, and *Peninsula Poets*.

171

She is at least thirty years old to be nesting and must weigh at least three hundred pounds. Her foreflippers are as long as my arms, thick and heavy looking, awkward on land. Her shell is round and shallow, similar in shape and size to a silver saucer my children use to slide on Michigan snow. The turtle strains and scrapes forward toward the distant sea grapes and grasses between the beach and buildings. She stops short of them. We walk close and form a silent semicircle around her like midwives within reach.

She begins to dig a hole. Over and over she sweeps sand behind herself, throws left, right, left, right, long high flipper tosses. The thumping of her shell reverberates the ground beneath my feet. It whumps rhythmically, then she rests.

Waves sip sand. I breathe in synchrony, stand motionless. In the long silent time she expels her eggs. I cannot see beneath her but know one hundred or more white eggs pass into the hole. She begins again to toss sand, creating a crest behind her, a smooth grainy dune. Twice she cried out a throaty turtle song then flailed and scraped and rocked her shell.

After an hour she is finished. She inches forward using her nose to press for balance, anchoring in as a climber uses crampons, legs pushing against the tension, heaving up from the hole. She pulls her way back to sea, melts into the night and surf and abandons the eggs. I follow the broad tracks until my feet get wet. She's vanished to deep water.

Her eggs will incubate for two months. The turtle embryos develop gender by temperature. The warmer eggs near the surface hatch females, the cooler, deeper eggs, males. If the nest is too shaded by tall buildings only males will develop. There are restrictions on building height in this area.

Free from their egg casings, hatchlings begin a fraternal frenzy of flippering to fan sand beneath themselves until they surface, usually before dawn. They instinctively break for the shimmer of light on the ocean, following the long erased tracks of their mother. Sea gulls, dogs, raccoons, and ghost crabs search them out. Of the more than ten thousand nests it is estimated only one thousand hatchlings will survive the land and sea predators in a season.

Later in the week, on our last day of freedom, my friends and I decide to rise early to do a predawn search for hatchlings. We dress, sip coffee, and rub on bug repellent. The air outside is moist, warm and still, the sky blue ink. We walk slowly down the sand coated stairway, past the grasses and sea grapes to the beach again in the dark. The ocean has a new rhythm this morning: a deeper, slower cadence, a sibilant rush, crash, smooth sweep, then a long pause before the next rush. Sand filters in my sandals as I sink-walk the dry grains. The wet sand by the ocean is smooth and even, it is like walking on brown sugar. By faint degrees the sky lightens. Here and there are remnants of seaweed, stringy sea litter and smoothed shells. Tiny holes spit and bubble in the ground after waves recede over them. A gull glides overhead. No hatchlings.

We walk easily together, quiet. A ghost crab scuttles across my path. A small burst of legs, slipping sideways then flitting sidewise in another direction, then vanishing. A phantom. A miniature monster with claws and pale body skittering at me, then away. A wide band of mauve appears at the horizon. The smooth roll of the ocean is iridescent, a color of pearl and light and liquid. Everywhere is quiet except for the insistent hush, rush of waves. Sunlight brightens the sky well before we see the ball roll from the sea like an overture.

We find exposed broken sea turtle eggs littered in a cluster, the hatchlings gone. No trail in the sand toward the ocean, only the tracks of a raccoon. No sign of struggle, only broken shells and paw prints.

What is it like to run the gauntlet to the sea when you are too young to understand the vulnerabilities but instinctively know to hurry, hurry, hurry toward the crashing wall? How large do waves sound? How much does a hatchling hear? Roar of water. A brother crunched whole. The click-skitter of a ghost crab.

We walk further along and sight another new nest where last night a large green laid her eggs. The hole is three feet deep and long enough to be a human grave. She must have been enormous. We turn back toward the condo. Tomorrow we all fly home to our families. The sun is past eye level; the blaze burns away the haze blurring the distant shoreline. We climb the sandy stairs, our shorts wet from surf. It is getting hot. The raccoons must be sleeping now, fat from their feed. A tender breakfast.

Lost Art:
Creating Intimacy Through Letter Writing

Kim Sanwald-Reimanis

What brings intimate communication to a soulful level? Honesty. Without honesty, we walk a dead-end road leading nowhere. The degree in which we stand within life's ambiguities and trust the process of intimacy, will be the degree to which we listen with our hearts and allow the opportunity for growth to occur.

Kim Sanwald-Reimanis has been an avid reader and writer all her life. She is particularly interested in the soulful quality and intimacy exchanged in letters between people reaching out to one another, and is developing a workshop to revive letter writing as an art form.

I believe we all carry a deep desire to communicate and connect. We are presented with a choice to see things through our own eyes or see things through the eyes of others. There is a longing to feel our uniqueness and bring this to bear in our everyday lives. Introspection and discernment are considered luxuries. Listening to our hearts is judged as weakness. We are encouraged to steel ourselves against an increasingly complicated world. This prevents us from diving deep below these surface emotions where our real gold lies.

We live in a society which expects quick answers and immediate clarity. We are given continuous, emotionally charged information and the judgment *du jour* with which to align ourselves. Right/wrong, black/white, we find security in tribal thinking. We may arrive at our judgments through our gender, our political affiliations, our religious background, our ethnicity or our experience. How do we arrive at a place that mellows these judgments and opens our hearts? How can we begin to slow things down and separate our emotional issues? What tools can we bring to aid the discovery of ourselves: what we think, how we feel? How do we bring forward a graceful, compassionate honesty, and communicate this to others?

Many people have sought meditation, prayer and solitude as ways to assist them in the recognition of their deeper-held truths. Within solitude and silence we find how many times we arrive at a place of both/and rather than either/or.

There is a forgotten tool available to us. Though slightly tarnished from lack of use, it is celebratory in nature. Exercising this forgotten tool will aid us in developing the art and craft of intimate expression. There is a significant difference between communicating data and expressing intimacy. This invaluable tool, the art of letter writing, will not only help us dive into the rich territory within us, but give us the means to express this beauty to others.

In the same way journaling provides a way into the self, letter writing provides a way of sharing intimacy. Letter writing is about intimacy. We choose our words with care. Thomas Moore shares with us in *Soul Mates,* "Something happens to our thoughts and emotions when we put them in a letter. They are placed in a different, special context, and they speak at a different level."

Letter writing is an exercise in self-development and sincerity. Differing from verbal discussions, where the energy of an individual's personality, or patterns of behavior can block our way, letters create the room needed for a more open and honest exchange. Letter writing is not about control or being careful. True intimacy is about exploration into deeper realms of communication, supported by solitude and a commitment to ourselves and to our *process* within our relationships.

Discovering honest and constructive ways to express intimacy teaches us new tools in sensitivity. We learn to speak from our heart, which allows us to temper our judgments. We develop new ways to communicate, allowing us to be empowered *with* other human beings rather than *over* them. We enter into relationships in a new way, allowing time to peel away each layer of emotion as it presents itself. We co-create environments where each of us takes the time to express a soulful experience uniquely inherent in the written. We call up realms of ourselves held silent when we engage in other mediums.

This is not unlike the process of listening to a familiar piece of music and picking up on a particular instrument or melody reaching you through a movement, or looking at a piece of art and acknowledging a feeling as you observe it. You may not be clear on what the artist intended, but we recognize something resonating inside ourselves in relationship to it. We have uncovered the lost art within the piece, within ourselves. It is the quality of this relationship that potentially holds deep and significant keys to understanding for each of us.

When we take time to explore our emotions through letter writing, we become more clear. The more we exercise this option, the more our self-esteem improves. This allows us to become better communicators, better intimates, better human beings.

This is where true intimate communication can take place, using language to convey these more expansive emotions on paper with heartfelt consideration. Letter writing can prove to be a true journey of discovery, bringing us closer to ourselves and each other. It is a journey of persistence, patience, and forgiveness, where we forge new meanings by slowing down and savoring each of our relationships as they unfold.

~~~

The following letter was written for my mother and read at her gravesite on
Mother's Day 1997:

Dear Mom,

Another Mother's Day approaches and I find myself staring out my living room window. Pink, yellow and white hyacinth bloom with brilliance along our sidewalk. I smile and receive spring's promise of rebirth.

Seven years have passed since your death and I sense a deep change occurring within. Although physically gone, you continue to be a presence in my life. I see you in unexpected glimpses through my relationships with others. Sometimes these reminders come unwelcomed. Other times they tug at my heart. Always they provide meaningful lessons. Our parting sent me on a journey of forgiveness and responsibility. I have prayed for clarity to understand and transcend my pain. I have harnessed the stubborn tenacity I learned from your example to chart a different course for myself.

Now, rather than wall myself from our similarities, I welcome them. I applaud my directness and feel free to speak my mind. I am learning to temper my bluntness by being respectful of others. Rather than let my fears control me and intimidate those around me, I use fear as a signpost to dig deeper in the understanding of myself.

My pain has taught me empathy and compassion for others in their life struggles. My isolation and depression have allowed me to embrace solitude as a teacher. I find myself thirsty for life, the moisture of which swells my heart as each drop finds me, until I am drenched and laughing. Joseph Campbell said, "Find a place where there is joy and the joy will burn out the pain."

How important to let love in. It shatters all our old boundaries and rigidities. It allows Mystery to be what it is. The Mystery of Love changes lives forever. When our paths cross again, I'm sure my soul will recognize the light within you.

How do I explain to you what you and our relationship have meant to me? I have written many letters to others with my heart spread all over them, and not once have I tried to convey to you how deeply you reside there. Love cannot be held back and still be called love. Love is not about being careful, rationing it out like a miser counts coins. In order for it to survive, it must be given and given freely.

I acknowledge our deep love for each other which was continually challenged by our similarities and passions. Rage, left unchecked, can be so unsympathetic. Though I am not a parent, I am a woman who nurtures both myself and others with great tenderness. I continue to be a work in progress. I am learning a love that tempers my judgments and opens my heart. I am keenly aware that before my soul can rest, I must accept your flaws as my own and hold them tenderly. They have been your greatest gifts.

When I look in the mirror and see your face, my eyes soften, and I see your secret poetry. I cannot forget you. Alice Walker said, "In search of my mother's garden, I found my own." You are always with me.

Much love,

Kim

Poetry

A Voices of Michigan Poet

Voices of Michigan

Grandpa Norman

Timothy Bunker is from Livonia, Michigan but was raised in nearby Novi. He
graduated from Western Michigan University. He is currently in charge of new
development for an automotive EDI and material release accounting package
for a software company.

Screw James Dean
Norman Rockwell lives at my house.
The old man with a twinkle in his eye, the young boys with
mischief in theirs.
Christmas scenes and the village square, white picket fences
and pretty little girls in summer dresses.
And the only rebel in the house is my dog who doesn't listen
to a damn thing I say.

My wife is not a model and she doesn't wear leather.
She'll spend her time in the garden, taking care of the
tomatoes and having coffee with the neighbors.
She doesn't need therapy and there isn't a hard edge to her.

It's the American dream, the one we had before our
misguided elders gave us their nightmare.
My world has more colors and less wires.
It doesn't mean we are simple or naive, it means we're happy
and content.
What is wrong with our world was not caused by us and will
not be solved by us.
But Mr. Rockwell will contribute a lot more than Mr. Dean.

- Timothy Bunker

Voices of Michigan

I'll See You Soon

Poetry has been the hobby and love of **E. Kay Mokma** since high school. Her poems are written from her life, her feelings, her experiences, and her observations. She writes for the pleasure and the insight which others may enjoy.

The elegantly white coifed lady in her pink pantsuit
Adjusts her walker as she plans her pursuit
Of an afternoon to spend with friends
With times to remember and to make amends.

Ah--there's Mary, my old friend with an ever warm smile.
With a cheering word to brighten your while
And turn a gloomy mood or a stormy day
To a pleasant one in her gentle way.
And a visit with Alice, what a dear.
She cared for her mother many a year.
And then, when her mother went--what a lonely life,
Even with rest at last, no cares, no strife.
And, Oh, my darling Henry, with so much love,
Always knowing whether I need a hug or a gentle shove.
And Maisie, and Ethel, and Freddie, and Sam--
Each one laughed with, or cried with, and so it ran.
And so the afternoon went,
And soon the sun was nearly spent.
"I must go now as my walk is slow."
As she got to the car feeling a lovely glow,
She turned and glanced slowly over the cemetery so,

185

And said to her friends, "I'll see you soon--
I'll see you soon."

And with a quiet smile she went to her home
To remember her time from her afternoon roam,
To her lonely meal, her lonely book, then her lonely bed.
And remembering again her long gone friends, she lay down
      her weary head,
And wistfully murmured--"I'll see you soon, maybe tonight.
I'll see you soon, perhaps by morning light."

- E. Kay Mokma

The Present

The way **Beth Herman** moves through the world has been deeply affected
by two things: time in nature and writing. Her writing is inspired by a desire
to communicate depth of feeling for people and issues that she is passionate
about. Writing serendipitously leads to deeper understanding and self-
growth.

A cluttered room with
wing-backed chairs, a piano and a
functional cuckoo clock-
That Christmas at my Grandmother's
twenty-one presents
were wrapped in hand-made
flannel pillowcases
because she thought
-as I think-
that it was wasteful to wrap in paper.
Being young, I didn't understand the weight
of the covering
and threw it aside in childish frenzy,
to seek my own fortune beyond the cover.
-I didn't notice the labor of the seams-

I have no recollection of what was inside
of my pillowcase
white with pink and blue poodles and bubbles printed on it.
The present is wrapped inside the soft, protective
piece of flannel

tucked in my chest.
I unearth it every year at this time and think of
her
and how, when little, sitting on her lap
I would mindlessly
stroke the back of her
worn hands.
How the flannel there was
soft and supple
-like my own-

As I struggle through carols on the piano
I think of how her life and death
has wrapped around, protected and rejoined
each one of us in the present-
Children, grandchildren, greats and great-greats
(four, thirteen, twenty and one).
How her spirit graces our annual
holiday gathering.
How she was the receptacle
that held,
still holds,
us all together.
How someday my baby may sleep on her cloth
and breathe the scent of her work
-dream her dreams-

Her layer of warmth and love
ever-holding the feathers for winged creatures inside.
Having flown far from her nest,
we live our lives

distant and hurried, compared to hers.
But every year we manage
to come together
and there is a sense that it is for her.
How else could we honor what she once instilled
in us
all of those years.

Protect your own.
Fly
but not so far that you forget where your
cover is.
Keep warm
              my dears
                        sleep tight.

- Beth Herman

Voices of Michigan

Losing Glass

Frank R. Jamison is a media manager and professor at Western Michigan University in Kalamazoo, Michigan, and has worked in the television field for the past 40 years. He has written numerous television and radio scripts, articles and monographs for professional publication and on subjects related to meditation and Buddhism.

There are many victims of glass in our world.
    I see now that I've been one.
Because it's transparent we don't notice.
    Looking around, though, it's everywhere.

How proud he must have been;
    That first Maker of Glass.
Life changed for him
    And those sharing his world.
Cooler, warmer . . . sanitary, durable,
    Ornamental, inexpensive.

For me it was there from the first -
    That maternity room observation window.
Aseptic as ever it could be
    In Independence, Missouri.
These things were important just before the war,
    When glass held so much of our future.

Never having been without
    I took it on.
Encased in glass and brick
    I watched in that house-of-home.
For every cue: "Behave like a little man."
    And men used glass!

Drove behind it, sat behind it,
    Polished it, framed it,
Won it at the movies,
    Ate on it, sometimes with it,
Spun it, heated it,
    Made it shatter-proof and heaped it, disposably.

So there I was, as you can see
    (And of course you can see, because of it),
In a world filled with glass.
    Never really thinking without it.
Assuming that without it the world
    Was too harsh for human commerce.

Until that day in Greeley, Colorado,
    When I took off work . . .
Left the office and went straight
    To the Suzuki shop,
"Just to look," I said to my friend, Dick Sorby.
    But he only smiled.
He was an artist and therefore mysterious.
    But mostly he was a Suzuki rider.

When I rolled that little machine
  Off the showroom floor
Glass began to fall away from my life.
  Not in jagged pieces, but like sand,
Easy on the wind.

So I rode with Dick.
  He showed me how to corner.
The gravel pits were my first classroom.
  Dick was a good friend.
As the glass came off my head.

We climbed every hill we could get to
  In Weld County.
The summer days of the high plains
  Were made for losing glass,
But only if you ride until you can't,
  And then stop by a shaded irrigation ditch
To cool the helmet sweat,
  Thinking about what is real.

And so I did. For a time
  The glass crackled and sparked.
Think how hard society's barriers can be.
  The noise and blood
Of my little personal war was horrendous.
  I could still show you scars.
On others, too, who were nearby.

Finally, though, the Suzuki 50
    Turned into a Honda 360.
The only glass covered the odometer,
    And not me.
Two cylinders are smoother than one
    In anybody's book.
And there's power to spare
    When you feel the need to move.

Facing eternity at every crossroad
    Makes a person think a lot about glass.
I've nearly frozen on 6 a.m. October rides
    In north Wisconsin.
My gloves have turned sweat dark in Indiana
    On horsefly afternoons.
But when they ask me, "Why not a windscreen?"
    I don't know how to make them hear.

Glass is either falling or forming
    Around each of us
As we motor along shimmering highways
    Toward mapless, wonderfilled tomorrows.

- Frank R. Jamison

Connection

Todd Alberda was born in Grand Rapids, Michigan. Throughout high school, she wrote poetry and won or placed in several local contests. In 1994 she graduated from Western Michigan University where she majored in French and English. Currently, she works for Stryker Medical in Kalamazoo.

--to my mother

We tug both ways
on the rope of what we
think is right
and say:
however much gathers
makes the other wrong.

Consider then this being right
means pulling others closer
by pushing oneself away,
so that even our differences
need us connected,
tied at the waist like this,
cord stretched between
as long as telephone wire,
brute tendril of common blood,
memory handed down.

It's when the slack's pulled taut
and drawn like a tightrope
through the years you lived
before I was born

that I think of this--
my love for you
looking back at me
still standing on the precipice,
I hesitate a little, breathe
then stepping free at last,
I balance across.

                    Todd Alberda

Statues of Children

The sculpted figures' curves
of tarnished bronze still luster
underneath the rain-crust.

The smothered shine of their faces
tell how long they've been here
cemented round the fountain at Bronson Park.

A circle of life-size children,
each piece fixed to a white stone base
still etched to fine detail:

holes in sneakers, tangled shoestrings
pleats in junior skirts and jeans;
their shins and knees are scabbed

as if their horseplay was really happening,
going on all the time,
though without any laughter,

without the tap and skip of jump rope
or the shuffle of hopscotch--
Pigtails shaking to heel-clicks,

without the fast pitch
flung with a huff
or the snap of the little glove

that catches it.
No luck of fun outside of that;
always caught somewhere between itch

and reaction, wind-up and release,
hammercock halfway to cap blast,
no matter how long the old brilliance takes

to fade completely from the surface.
Lucky for that, then, no metal
could ever give the children life,

nor mineral duplicate their sentience so well
that one couldn't tell them apart;
no hammer and chisel

working however long or hard
can chip off enough stone that isn't the child
and no heart will awaken.

- Todd Alberda

Recovery

Betty Lou Cooke is an Information Technology writer and editorial consultant with more than twenty-five years of professional experience in marketing communications. As a freelance non-fiction writer, her subjects cover a broad range of fine contemporary crafts. She recently returned after fifty years to her home state of Michigan.

I heard the howl --
some animal whose pain
tore whole its tongue
and flung its moan along the hollow corridors
until it found my room
and swallowed me.
And only as I lay engulfed
was I to know
the mouth was mine.

- Betty Lou Cooke

Voices of Michigan

Vidiots

"**Doc**" spends his summers on Mackinac Island, Michigan.

Vidiots!
Tuneslave automobilists.
Stoplighting.
Fastforwarding.
Running on empty.
Speed reading the poetry of life.
Made vain and plain
By being entertained,
Exit your entrancement!

Vidiots!
Tuneslave tele-mongerers.
Ditto-ing the ditties
That hum in your heads.
Bumpersticker speaking,
Sermonizing sound bytes,
Fast fooding the feast of life.
Explained and constrained
By being entertained,
Exit your entrancement!

Vidiots!
Tuneslave gadget-gropers.
Doting on the dotted line,
Dialing for dollars,
Rumplestilt-spinning
The wheels of fortune.
Super-malled by marketing bears.
Thinking tinkling trinkets
The priceless gifts of life.
Obtained and restrained
By being entertained,
Exit your entrancement!

Vidiots!
Tuneslave cyber-cyphers.
Hard-driving the infomercial tollways.
Re-recording your pre-planned experiences,
Snap-shooting your hip images,
Cataloging for home, shop, and office
Networks, your virtual realities.
C/d rom-ing the mysteries of life.
Trained to be sustained
By being entertained,
Exit your entrancement!

Vidiots!
Tuneslave,
Tele-groping,
Auto-gadgeteers.
Constrained to be plain.
Trained to be vain.
Fully explained.
Routinely obtained.
Daily restrained.
Completely sustained
By being entertained,
Exit your entrancement!

Turn it off!
Turn it allll off!
And get off-
On the poetic mystery,
The priceless gift,
The feast of life!

- "Doc"

Voices of Michigan

Scenes from the Porch

Caitlin Taylor wrote *Scenes* during the first of her three summers as houseparent for the Mackinac Island State Park, and sequels became annual events. Her affliction with Mackinac Magic is considered permanent. Jubilantly so.

Weathered grey boards take the walk from "women's quarters" to "men's." Steps reach down to grassy earth -- and days band into weeks, weeks bind into months -- and in these days and nights and weeks, four dozen heartbeats take turns lining these weathered steps -- and what goes there bands them into comrades, binds them into friends:

I.   Tree limbs bow and blow
         toss and shiver.
         If you lie still enough beneath them
         you can enter each tree's song.

II.   Billow-skirted wenches bob across the green --
         wending gaily to work. How pretty they are --
         gathered into yards of fabric, hair gathered in, too.
         Not gathered is the chatter, and the laughter --
               that scatters in their wake.

III.   A flutter of white grazes
         the water's blue.
         A heart lifts inside the white body, gliding --
         and so does mine.

IV.   They return -- aprons sooted, strands of lively hair
escaping, lips pearled with sweat.
The stride is weary, the chatter quelled.
Yet eyes still sparkle as they lift skirts to show off
ruffled pantaloons and stockinged-ankles to the
ever-approving men.

V.   A splat of monarch butterfly pastes itself
to the white clapboard side of Mission House.
Wee grey friend-mouse scoots from his
bottom-step-den, and peers about.

VI.   Man carries laundry down.
Woman reads newspaper.
Man passes woman reading newspaper,
not carrying laundry.
Woman smokes.
Man carries laundry up.
Man smokes.
Man smoking speaks to woman reading newspaper.
Woman laughs.
Woman smiles at man carrying laundry.
Man smiles back.
The Passing of the Laundry Brigade.

VII.   One night's thunder drenches the sky all around
with arced fire.
Bolt after bolt wakes the rainy night-sky into day.

VIII.   Bikes zip.
        Halloo's holler.
        Hands wave.
        Smiles burst.

IX.   Evening, soft as rain, billows up the grassy slope
                and folds around us all.
        The water glides from blue, to smoke, to pewter, to
                dusk.
        Stars sprout in the deepening sky.
        Bats bloom to whiz and whisper, adding shroud to
                the night.
        A single star slides across an arc of sky, and winks
                out.
        Someone leans into a guitar -- and pours music on
                us all.

                        - Caitlin Taylor

Voices of Michigan

The Porch Swing

Erynne M. Rice is a sophomore at North Central Michigan College where she is working toward an elementary education degree. She enjoys reading and many outdoor activities. Erynne has no formal writing history, and this is her first entry in a contest or publication.

Back and forth, the sway of the porch swing,
as two lovers cling for the last time,
trying to get their fill until the next time they meet.

Best friends rock back and forth spilling secrets,
as fast as they can. Gossip back and forth,
delighting in the knowledge of the true friendship they share.

Tears fall on the lonely swing,
the wood absorbing the pain the occupant brings in quiet
understanding,
swaying back and forth bringing comfort to whose heart is
breaking.

Family gatherings are a fine affair, but those who seek the
quiet,
go and find the swing, for it's always there,
soaking in the night air, peace descends filling the void.

Two parents sit and swing, watching
as their daughter leaves home for the first time
with a mixture of pain and relief, hoping that they did the
right thing.

Calm sets over the house, as they watch
a young robin jump from the branches,
and spread its wings.

Years come and go, the swing sits empty, for nobody's
home.
The marks of history the swing still bears,
for it was always there.

- Erynne M. Rice

A Remembered Valentine

Tamera Jo Sylvester has been a Head Start teacher for the past twelve years. She has two teenage children and chose to raise them in Hillsdale County. She has never written professionally though she has always loved writing. She finds writing poems a quiet, peaceful, and satisfying pastime.

Hearts, glitter, glue, crayons, paper,
scissors, paint, ribbons.
LOVE.
How very special a paper heart can make
a person feel.
My favorite Valentine is tucked away in
my memory box, stashed under flowers and
invitations.
Stuck between booties and certificates
is a paper doily folded in half.
It has shiny red heart stickers placed
about it with a lopsided purple heart
crayoned in the center.
Glitter was painstakingly placed around
the edges in great globs.
Ribbons were cut so the fraying ends
would hang off the paper in three foot
streamers.
There were no words written on the
paper, but I recall the beautiful
memories of receiving that particular
Valentine every time I open it.

211

A smile came to my face as two tiny
gluey hands presented this work of love to me.
The anticipation of making it, the
impatience of waiting for it to dry, the
excitement of the giving were all quite
evident in the huge dark lashed eyes
that were looking at me.
Hallmark has nothing over the purest,
proudest love of a child.
The hug I received that day was like no
other, tiny sticky fingers on my face,
in my hair, around my neck.
I pulled my little cherub into my lap
and examined each red heart, every mark
of the crayon, each piece of ribbon.
"What does it say?" I asked my sweet
child.
Impishly he replied, "I love you, momma."

- Tamera Jo Sylvester

Where I Am Not

Becky Thomas, a senior at Western Michigan University, is studying
secondary education with an English major and minors in history and music.
Her publications include *I Was Told to Write a Poem* and *The High School
Writer.*

---

sailboats
Marquette Park
bustling tourists
flags unfurling in the summer wind
What I should be seeing
Where I am not.

clip-clop of horses' hooves
booming cannons
airhorns of ships
the sounds of a million different languages
What I should be hearing
Where I am not.

breathe in deeply
fudgeicecreamhorsemanure
the unique aroma
What I should smell
Where I am not.

the fort
military music

213

historic buildings
limestone landmarks
I can touch the past
Where I am not.

cool breezes
whispered songs of friendship
echoing forever
the laughter of
Where I belong
Where I am not.

- Becky Thomas

The Old Tree by the Road

Margaret **VanderVeen**, a native of Portage, Michigan, is married with four
children and four grandchildren. She is an avid reader, sports fan and
nature lover. She spends a lot of time at her cabin in Baldwin by the Pere
Marquette River. She studied writing and literature at Western Michigan
University and the University of Michigan and has been published.

Once she stood so tall and proud
On a hill on my grandfather's farm.
The horses huddled beneath her for shade
As they came from their stalls in the barn.

I clearly remember calling the cows
On an Indian Summer night.
The sound of tinkling bells in the breeze
And the hint of an early moonlight.

Do you think a tree can cry,
Do you think she feels the pain?
Does she cry, like me, for what was then,
Does she cry for what might have been?

For the long stemmed cattails growing tall
Where the red-winged blackbirds preened,
For the peaceful pond where the animals drank,
Where the Will-O-The-Wisp was seen.

Now the dozers have leveled the hills
And the pond and marshes are filled,
And the Sun blazes on Highway 131
And the barn and the farmhouse are gone.

What it took my grandfather's family to build
Was lost in a few, brief days.
Two hundred years of history erased
In the path of a bulldozer's blade.

Now all that remains is the Oak Tree
That stands by the side of the road.
The masses speed by and they never know why
She's out there...all alone.

- Margaret VanderVeen

Western Avenue

Since childhood **Darryl C. Stiles** has been a frustrated writer. Now in her dotage years she has finally found time to take a creative writing class at Gogebic Community College in Ironwood, stirring her desire to follow her dreams.

I remember my home where I grew up
On Western Avenue, at the end of the broken sidewalk.
Sitting on the front steps, telling fairy tales
To the neighborhood children,
Who sat with me on the hot, summer evenings
In Detroit, dreaming of places far from Western Avenue,
With its box like houses, row on row,
From Michigan Avenue to the railroad tracks,
At the end of the street.

I remember walking along the railroad tracks
On cold winter days, picking up coal,
To burn in the stove.

We were all poor on Western Avenue,
During the Depression,
It was no disgrace picking up coal.

- Darryl C. Stiles

Voices of Michigan

A View of Mackinac Bridge

Marla Kay Houghteling was born and raised in Michigan, but lived in
Pennsylvania for 25 years before returning to Michigan in 1996. She writes
poems, essays and short stories. Her work has appeared in *The Christian
Science Monitor, Ellery Queen's Mystery Magazine, The Writer,* and *Passages
North.*

Behind the dryer's porthole,
my clothes began a sluggish journey
out of heavy wetness.
A rooster of a man,
his plaid flannel buttoned up
to his pleated neck,
perched next to me
on the yellow plastic chair.

He ignored the piles of battered
Time and *Newsweek*
and the book waiting in my lap
as he launched long sentences
from between clicking dentures.
His eyes held the blue of the Big Lake
with its first skim of ice.

He is up on a catwalk
over the Straits in '54, or was it '55?
in the November night.
The cables creak; the feeble lights

of the night shift are swallowed
by the dark wind.
The fellow next to him
loses his fragile footing
and goes over, his cry
trailing behind him like a scarf.

Above the dryers' roar,
buttons click against
metal innards.
Sleeves reach out for purchase,
pants legs twist in a dark wind.

                              - Marla Kay Houghteling

The Soo

Let me finish here,
then go to Sault Ste. Marie
and sit on a bench
as the sun sets
on the Canadian side.

I'll watch the man
who sweeps up
the tourists' butts
rest his broom against a tree
and feed a squirrel
corn from his pocket.

And I will never tire of seeing
the ships fall and rise
as they wait patiently
in the locks, wanting
to get to the other lake
but knowing that stopping
is part of the journey.

- Marla Kay Houghteling

Voices of Michigan

222

the foolish travelers

Thirty miles from Sault Ste. Marie and a bike ride from Lake Superior,
Stefanie L. Moran and her husband Terry are pursuing their dream of living
a simple, basic life. It is here that Stefanie, age 26, is inspired to write about
a way of life few will ever know.

she travels along
with leash in hand
and never a place to be,

the neighbors laugh
at her foolishness
and wonder when she'll see-

that the turtle she walks
covers a trail
far below a human's measure,

and that her slow friend
holds her back from
discovering worldly pleasure.

she travels along
with leash in hand
and never a place to be,

she laughs at the neighbors'
foolishness

and wonders when they'll see-
that she walks her turtle
to keep it slow
not caring what distance it measures,

not having to walk from
her own back yard
to discover life's little pleasures.

- Stefanie L. Moran

Young Woman

Melinda Hare is a sixth grade teacher at Hastings Middle School. She also helps with the high school marching band's color guard in the fall, the ski club in the winter, and the girls' middle school track team in the spring. Melinda enjoys pottery, running, biking, skiing, and reading.

Get out young woman.
Free yourself.
Run young woman.
Find your inner peace.
Laugh young woman.
Be the one you want to be.
Be strong young woman.
Stick to your convictions.
Keep safe young woman.
Take care of you first.
Push hard young woman.
Reach the top of the hill.
Stand tall young woman.
Look above what's left behind.
Swing high young woman.
Reach for the sky.

- Melinda Hare

Living Life

Feeling the sun on your face.
Seeing the flowers in bloom with dancing butterflies.
Getting a phone call from someone who just wanted to say
hi.
Taking a nap when you need to.
Eating because it tastes good.
Running for your heart.
Reading for your mind.
Praying for your soul.
Loving yourself and others unconditionally.
Receiving that same kind of love.
Riding for the fun of it.
Standing on your own.
Speaking the truth.
Knowing that this is what life is about.

- Melinda Hare

Michigan Morning

Hazelruth Winters has compiled a book of over two hundred poems. She is
an active member of her church, an art teacher and a professional artist.
She reads her poems at Gospel Sings and other places in Michigan and is
published by *The National Library of Poetry*.

The hues of pink and purple
Let me know that spring is here
A beautiful Michigan sunrise
What a lovely time of the year
All of Gods' creations
Are coming back alive
The flowering of the apple tree
And the buzzing of the hive
The geese are honking loudly
While flying over head
I listen to the croaking frogs
While lying in my bed
A little robin comes to nest
Upon my window pane
His happy song fills my heart
While I listen to the rain
Far off on a pine tree branch
Owl let's us know he's there
With apple blossoms all around
There fragrance fills the air
What a wonderful land this is
With all the beauty to see
It seems as though God made it all
Just for you and me

- Hazelruth Winters

227

Voices of Michigan

Intimacy

Michael Nagrant aspires to be a screenwriter, folk guitarist, and President of the United States. Otherwise he will be happy traveling in search of dead heroes and a private audience with Ani Difranco. Originally from Shelby Township, Michigan, he is a poet who has been published.

I sulked there naked
on the window sill
clothed in the fashions
of clock tower shadows
and accessorized
by the city lights burning brilliantly.

Hot in the melting night
A brutal promiscuous gaze
gave proof to your devious ways
sparing no moment for insecurity.

You had many boxes
behind you on the burnished bureau.
Chinese porcelain embedded with wisdom
Exotically   silk woven
Stoically   wooden
Ironically   plastic
and Fragile   paper maché.

You had so many boxes
I wanted to peek in each.
As I opened the one you had always kept,
you said it was the first you had been given.

I had held many boxes
but none before had I touched with
the hesitancy of inflamed flesh.

- Michael Nagrant

The Barn

Christina-Marie Umschied, born in Weiden, West Germany was raised in Saint Louis, Missouri and has lived in Petoskey, Michigan since 1976. Publications include magazines such as: *Chicago Review, Hiram Poetry Review, Odyssey, Negative Capability, Great Lakes Review, Huron Review, The Mac Guffin, Sou'Wester, Great Midwestern Quarterly,* and e-zine, *World Poetry.*

The barn sags in the middle,
an old woman's breast.
I remember fullness and cow's milk
I remember old brown boards
hugging against blizzards
instead of jagged teeth, crooked
teeth, teeth that let winter grin
through cracks.

Within these walls
the sun pretends spring.
Light peers through in circles
and I hide from sunlight fire
that has blackened corners.
I will not be touched
not even by my own hands.

Look at these hands that
are as brown as the barn.
Skin papers over disappearing bones.
On this parchment is written my years.

The first ten years clutched a swing,
flying back and forth from
now to the future. Look at these scars
that mark my first love.
Look at the rings that left me here.
And wrinkles that gave birth,
between wrenching lives from wombs and
wrenching corn from yellowed stalk.

"Look," I scream into silence.
All I hear is the barn creaking bones,
and gulls so far in the distance,
they sound like church bells.

- Christina-Marie Umschied

Right Here at Home

Doris Kennard was born in Saginaw, Michigan, graduated from Arthur Hill High School and attended the New York School of Interior Design. Doris is a retired business owner and has had poems published in *Iliad Press, Sparrowgrass, Saginaw News, Tuscola Advertiser and Vassar Pioneer Times.*

I have not strolled the Champs Elysees
Nor seen the moon on Galway Bay.
The Sphinx my eyes have not beheld
Nor have I sailed an ocean swelled.
Yet I have seen the morning break
Right here at home on Murphy Lake.
The Seven Wonders Of The World
If all before me were unfurled,
I doubt could make my pulse race more
Than sunrise on her Eastern shore.
If pocketbook my fate decree
That I no world-wide traveler be,
Proclaims my fate be not to roam,
Then I shall be content at home
To watch the sunrise paint new days
Her gentle hills, her sky and bays.
My joyful heart glad praise will lift
To God for this most precious gift:
The chance to see the morning break
Right here at home on Murphy Lake.

- Doris Kennard

Voices of Michigan

234

The Nest

Keith N. Dusenberry lives in Troy, Michigan but spends eight months per year forty-two minutes away at the University of Michigan-Ann Arbor. An English major enamored of Beat Generation writers Jack Kerouac and Allen Ginsberg, Keith enjoys playing music and driving his Volkswagen Bus. He plans to become an English Professor.

I got up in the middle of the night
And looked out my window.
Saw the remains of 3-day old snowfall
And thought how much my front lawn
Looked like the surface of the moon.
Craters where feet had been,
Some small from the little crater-maker next door
And some big, possibly my own.
The dark side on the far side of
The large maple tree,
And the Sea of Tranquility
Reflecting moonlight on the window pane.
And I thought how free I truly am,
And at the same time, how alone we all are;
Though we hide from it with our
Inter-Planetary Dating Service.
So I looked up at the celestial moon
And down at my earthen moon,
And then I took a step.

- Keith N. Dusenberry

Rounder Records

The young yearn for seniority
As the old grasp at youth
And they meet at a junction
Between understanding
And embarrassment,
Only to find they are exactly
What they vowed never to become.

- Keith N. Dusenberry

Barn Dance

Shelley A. Topham is a student at Saginaw Valley State University majoring in Communication with a minor in Creative Writing. Shelley has works published by Green Gate Publishing as well as the National Library of Poetry.

The rhythmic ticking
of the tack room marble mantle clock
canters like a wild mustang on the run.

The metal hands
hold onto the weathered reins
with passion.

The split-rail fence
leans against
the sun's shadow.

The rusty sleigh bells slumber
within the walls
of the collapsing barn.

The soil settles
in the nostrils
of all who plow its fields.

Calloused hands
count the speckled seeds,
exhaling a cloud of cotton breath.

A grey milk bucket
hangs on a hook
above the wooden stairs.

A sparrow
fills it with
harvested straw.

The empty tree swing
waltzes
with the wind.

I dance bare-footed
in the light
of the full moon

As I
curtsy to the
drunken daisies.

- Shelley A. Topham

Virtual Reality

Jeaneene Nooney has written poems, essays, and short stories, primarily in the genre of Christian literature and nature writing. She's a wife, mother of three, and lives in the northern Michigan woods. "Into our seemingly ordinary lives, God gives us glimpses of eternity. I try to evoke that in my writing."

Plight of children
       lesson learned;
Mom is busy
       love is spurned.

Moving image
       hook me in
lose me where
       they can't come in.

My family is the
       one in there
where Dad is home
       and Mom will care.

It's true they
       cannot hold me tight
and tell me everything's
       all right.

I understand,
        like Dad and Mom,
they're not trying to be mean.
            They just can't leave the screen.

- Jeaneene Nooney

The Weaning

"Too soon," I said,
"O God!"
"You took my dad
too young.
Deprived him of his
grandchildren;
sweet anthems left unsung."

"You took him ere
I had the chance
to curse the world
with him.
Before our viewpoints
merged at all,
before I cherished him."

"My child," you said,
"His time to leave
was consummately planned
to stir your soul
to higher things
to wean you from
the things at hand."

An eaglet satisfied
with earthy nest
gives not to flight

241

her earnest best,
till heavenward father
bids her come
to soar on heights
as yet unknown.

~~~

But I have stilled and quieted my soul;
Like a weaned child with its mother,
Like a weaned child is my soul within me.
Psalm 131:2

- Jeaneene Nooney

Appendices

Arch Rock

Voices of Michigan

The Artists

The sketches featured in *Voices of Michigan* are from a Mackinac Island sketchbook by **Rob Harrell** a freelance illustrator located in Indianapolis, Indiana. To see more of Rob's work, please visit his website, www.RobHarrell.com.

The oil painting used for the cover of *Voices of Michigan* was done by **Marlee Musser** who was raised in Petoskey on the shore of Lake Michigan. Marlee's paintings hang in many private and corporate collections in the US and abroad, most notably in Washington, DC, at the White House. Marlee works on location, and in her studio at her home on Mackinac Island, where she lives with her husband, Dan Musser and daughter, Amelia.

The cover for *Voices of Michigan* was designed by **Cecilia Winston-Floren**, artist, photographer, writer and musician who lives and works in the Hudson Valley of New York near Ossining. She owns a small business, CECI GRAPHICS, which deals in computer and conventional graphic design and illustration, and SeeTheeEarth greeting cards which incorporate both photographs and pen and ink prints. Contact Ceci at: qverencia@aol.com.

West Bluff

The Publishers

Mary Jane Barnwell and **Jane Harrell Winston** met on Mackinac Island, Michigan a short time ago and discovered they both shared a dream. Mary Jane was interested in publishing a book; Jane was interested in conducting a writing contest. And thus began *Voices of Michigan... an Anthology of Michigan's Finest New Authors.* A publishing company was needed, so they decided to form their own. They combined Mackinac and their names and became MackinacJane's Publishing Company. The rest is what is known as "history." It is hoped that you, the authors, and you the consumers enjoy the book and the writings within as much as Mary Jane and Jane have enjoyed running the contest and publishing the book.

Mary Jane, a Michigander born in Detroit, spent summers on Mackinac Island. She has degrees in Nutrition from Northern Michigan and Wayne State Universities and currently she and husband, Roman, and their three-year-old son, Willie, live in Petoskey. Mary Jane co-owns and helps manage the Island Bookstores of Mackinac Island and Mackinaw City. A lover of book selling, she always wanted to be involved in the publishing of a book. Realizing she would never be a published author, she decided she could help others fulfill their dreams to become published authors.

Jane, born and reared in Bloomington, Indiana, married an Air Force officer after graduating from Indiana University and traveled with John and Uncle Sam for the next 30 years. They currently live in Warner Robins, Georgia in the winter and on Mackinac Island, Michigan in the summer. Jane is a faculty member of Fort Valley State University in Fort Valley, Georgia where she teaches in the College of Education. A grown daughter, Jamie Sue Stanzione, a grown son, John Jeffrey Winston, six grandchildren and two cats round out the Winston household.

The Readers/Judges

Jean Beardsley Allen, a published author with three books to her credit: *The Threads of Time, Mystery of Messiah* and *It's Fun To Live on Mackinac Island,* has a Master of Arts from Michigan State University and taught in the Michigan public schools for 21 years. At one time very active in the Mackinac Island Chamber of Commerce, she now spends her summers on Mackinac Island, Michigan and her winters in Sarasota, Florida.

Lorabeth Fitzgerald grew up in Hillsdale, Michigan where her love affair with words began early. As a child she put out a neighborhood newspaper; she was the editor of her high school newspaper and went on to become the editor of *The Flat Hat* at the College of William and Mary in Virginia where she concentrated in English literature. Following University she worked as a newspaper reporter, in the editorial offices of *Coronet* and *Esquire* magazines in New York City, as the Information Services Officer of Michigan State University and ultimately taught high school English.

Virginia Garland, born and reared in Evansville, Indiana, is a graduate of the University of Evansville with a Bachelor and Master of Science in Education and has completed all requirements for her principal's certification from Indiana State University in Terre Haute, Indiana. Virginia is currently employed by the Evansville Unified School District of Evansville, Indiana at Vogel Elementary School as a fifth grade teacher.

Kay Beth Harrell, a native of Sedalia, Missouri and a graduate of the University of Missouri's School of Journalism worked as a continuity writer for KCMO-AM, FM and TV in

Kansas City, Missouri, wrote advertising for KTBC-TV in Austin, Texas and was a correspondent for United Press International in the capital bureau in Austin. In recent years she has worked on several books that have been published by the Monroe County, Indiana Historical Society. She and her husband have a summer home on Mackinac Island, Michigan.

Dr. Chris Hauge is in private practice as a clinical therapist and hypnotherapist in Wilmington, North Carolina where he retired after ten years active duty in the US Air Force. He holds his Doctor of Social Work and Master of Social Work degrees plus a Bachelor Degree in Secondary Education from the University of Utah. He serves as an adjunct instructor in the Master in Counseling Program at Webster University in Myrtle Beach, South Carolina and at the University of North Carolina in Wilmington where he conducts group therapy.

Donald P. McGraw III, a resident of Warner Robins, Georgia, is a man of many talents. He is an accomplished playwright as well as an accomplished director who enjoys directing what he writes as well as what others write. An editorial columnist for a newspaper in the Knight-Ridder family, Don has also begun a poetry web site. A graduate of Mercer University in Macon, Georgia with a Bachelor of Arts in English and Philosophy, Don was a former high school English teacher, mental health counselor, and now serves as a probation officer.

Diane Orth and husband Bill live in Boise, Idaho. Diane was born in a small town in southern Washington State and attended Washington State University. She has lived in several parts of the country and has had several different careers including owning an employment agency, but for the past 17 years she has served as Director of Relocation for real estate firms.

Janet Rathke, our Duluth, Minnesota reader, was raised in Jackson, Michigan, once lived with her husband and son in Charlevoix, loves Mackinac Island and visits there as often as possible. She learned of the contest through the Mackinac Island newspaper *The Town Crier*. Janet has a BS in Home Economics Education and a Master of Arts degree in Guidance and Counseling both from Eastern Michigan University in Ypsilanti. She has worked for the Cooperative Extension Service in Michigan, Minnesota and Wisconsin. Currently she is employed with Barnes and Noble and Mary Kay Cosmetics.

Barbara Jane Schroeder, a resident of Central Lake, Michigan, is married with two children and two grandchildren. She attended George Washington University, is a member of the Junior League of Flint and Birmingham, Michigan and has served as an active volunteer no matter where she lives. Husband, Chuck, has recently retired and they now have big plans of wintering in Florida.

Doyle Spence, a born-and-reared Georgian, is basking in the success of his first published collection of poetry, *Shades of Conscience*, which was released in September, 1997. About his collection he says, "these are poems that make you sit down and think." Although his passion is poetry and has been since he was 12, he is also interested in fiction, mysteries, suspense, biographies and especially loves the study of history.

Bonnie Sperry earned her Bachelor and Master of Arts in English from Indiana University in Bloomington, Indiana. She took her teaching expertise to Balboa Island, California after graduation, but while there yearned for the mid-west. She returned to and currently lives in Bloomington, Indiana

249

where she taught junior high English for a number of years. She has, however, traded "shaping young minds" for "caring for seven Old English Sheep dogs, one Bearded and one Border Collie" she and husband Phil have graciously adopted from the Indianapolis Humane Society!

Dr. Francis (Fran) H. Straus II, a professor in the Department of Pathology in the College at the University of Chicago, has medical licensure in Illinois as well as Michigan. Fran spends portions of his summers on Mackinac Island where he pursues his avocations of reading and writing history. Frank has two published books, written 11 textbook chapters, 89 scientific papers, 45 abstracts, two book reviews and two letters to the editor!

Janice Trollinger is a member of the English faculty at Fort Valley State University, a small historical black school of approximately 3,000 students which is a part of the University System of Georgia. Her degrees include a Bachelor of Arts in English and a Master of Arts in English from the University of Missouri. Janice, a prolific conference presenter on topics involving writing, has had a number of professional journal articles published through the years.

Glen Young, a high school English teacher in Alanson, Michigan, is a graduate of the University of Michigan. He is a past recipient of a National Endowment for the Humanities research fellowship; his literary reviews have appeared in the National Council of Teachers of English publication *The English Journal* and are destined to appear elsewhere in the future. He spends his summers on Mackinac Island with his wife and two children where they operate The Surrey Sandwich shop.

Permission was granted by the following authors for publication of their listed work(s) in this first edition of **Voices of Michigan.**

Alberda, Todd: *Statues of Children/Connection.*
Anderson, Erin: *Doing Time.*
Andree, Maralee: *Cub Scouts and Other Oaths.*
Baker, Constance M: *Seascapes:*A Compilation of Essays
Ball, Millie: *A Golden Summer.*
Beaty, Anne: *Scenes from a Classroom.*
Boyer, Marion: *Shoreleave.*
Braun, Philip J: *The Time We Invited Ann Sheridan.*
Bunker, Timothy: *Grandpa Norman.*
Cooke, Betty Lou: *Recovery.*
"Doc": *Vidiots.*
Dusenberry, Keith N: *Rounder Records/The Nest.*
Flaig, Bonnie: *An Instinct for Grief.*
Hare, Melinda A: *Young Woman/Living Life.*
Herman, Beth D: *The Present.*
Hoover, Tom: *King of the Forest.*
Houghteling, Marla Kay: *A View From Mackinac Bridge/Soo.*
Jamison, Frank R: *Losing Glass.*
Kennard, Doris: *Right Here At Home.*
Kenyon III, John H: *Virgin in the Volkswagen Bus.*
Lein, Noah: *The Wreck of the Savior.*
McGleish, Maurice C: *Antlers in the Treetop.*
Mokma, E. Kay: *I'll See You Soon.*
Moran, Stefanie L: *the foolish travelers.*
Nagrant, Michael J: *Intimacy.*
Nooney, Jeaneene L: *Virtual Reality/The Weaning.*
Rice, Erynne M: *The Porch Swing.*
Robinson, Laura: *Remembrances.*
Sanwald-Reimanis, Kim: *Lost Art:Creating Intimacy Through Letter Writing.*
Snider, Ann M: *Love Unending.*
Stiles, Darryl: *Western Avenue.*
Sylvester, Tamera Jo: *A Remembered Valentine.*
Taylor, Catlin: *Scenes from the Porch.*
Thomas, Becky: *Where I am Not.*
Thornburg, Fred: *'Ig 'Oy.*
Topham, Shelley A: *Barn Dance.*
Umschied, Christina-Marie:*The Barn.*
VanderVeen, Margaret Ann: *The Old Oak Tree.*
Walsh, Rita: *The Carp in the Pool.*
Wennerberg-DuFay, Angela L: *The Answer is in the Skyline.*
Winters, Hazelruth: *Michigan Morning.*

Voices of Michigan

252

Voices of Michigan

Voices of Michigan order information:
ISBN 0-9667363-0-3

*Fax orders: 1 (616) 348-5265
*Telephone orders: Call Toll Free: 1 (877) 487-1098 or
                                        1 (616) 487-1098
*E-mail orders: Macjanes@juno.com
*Postal orders:

> **MackinacJane's Publishing Company**
> *Voices of Michigan*
> 115 State Street
> Petoskey, MI 49770

Pricing:
*Book price $15.95
*Michigan Sales Tax 6% (No tax when shipping out of MI)
*Shipping and handling $4.00. [Add $.96 tax and $1.00
     shipping and handling for each additional book.]
     Total for one book: $20.91

Payment:
□ Check
□ Credit card: □ MasterCard □ VISA
Card number: _____
Name on card: _____
Expiration date: _____

Ship to:
Name: _____
Address: _____
City, State and Zip _____
Phone number (   ) _____

Voices of Michigan may also be purchased at your local bookstore.